The Analytic-Synthetic Distinction

Basic Problems in Philosophy Series

A. I. Melden and Stanley Munsat
University of California, Irvine
General Editors

Human Rights
A. I. Melden

Guilt and Shame
Herbert Morris, University of California, Los Angeles

The Analytic-Synthetic Distinction
Stanley Munsat

Civil Disobedience and Violence
Jeffrie G. Murphy, University of Arizona

Morality and the Law
Richard A. Wasserstrom, University of California, Los Angeles

War and Morality
Richard A. Wasserstrom

The Analytic-Synthetic Distinction

Edited by

Stanley Munsat

University of California, Irvine

Wadsworth Publishing Company, Inc., Belmont, California

ISBN–0–534–00042–8
L. C. Cat. Card No. 76–165002

Printed in the United States of America

1 2 3 4 5 6 7 8 9 10—76 75 74 73 72 71

Series Foreword

The Basic Problems in Philosophy Series is designed to meet the need of students and teachers of philosophy, mainly but not exclusively at the undergraduate level, for collections of essays devoted to some fairly specific philosophical problems.

In recent years there have been numerous paperback collections on a variety of philosophical topics. Those teachers who wish to refer their students to a set of essays on a specific philosophical problem have usually been frustrated, however, since most of these collections range over a wide set of issues and problems. The present series attempts to remedy this situation by presenting together, within each volume, key writings on a single philosophical issue.

Given the magnitude of the literature, there can be no thought of completeness. Rather, the materials included are those that, in the judgment of the editor, must be mastered first by the student who wishes to acquaint himself with relevant issues and their ramifications. To this end, historical as well as contemporary writings are included.

Each volume in the series contains an introduction by the editor to set the stage for the arguments contained in the essays and a bibliography to help the student who wishes to pursue the topic at a more advanced level.

A. I. Melden
S. Munsat

Stanley Munsat is an Associate Professor of Philosophy at the University of California, Irvine. He received a B.A. degree from Cornell University, and an M.A. and Ph.D. from the University of Michigan. He has published *The Concept of Mind* (1967) and articles in several journals, including *Mind* and *American Philosophical Quarterly*.

Preface

This volume is designed to introduce the issues surrounding the analytic-synthetic distinction; the germinal writings on the topic are presented from a historical perspective for use in introductory and intermediate courses. Also included as critical aids to the reader are Pap's elegant treatment of the all-important selection from Kant and Frege's witty critical review of the major historical positions on the nature of mathematical truth. The Frege piece should also help the reader see some of the requirements for an adequate theory of mathematical truth (historically one of the key testing points for an account of the varieties of truth).

In the textual material footnotes are original; in some cases they have been deleted. Deletions in the text, within a single section, are indicated by ellipses.

I would like to thank Professors Karel Lambert and Gordon Brittan, the University of California, Irvine, and Wallace I. Matson, University of California, Berkeley, for their valuable comments, and Gordon Brittan for suggestions on format. In addition, I wish to thank Barbara Ellerbrock who typed the manuscript and Lisa Munsat who edited and typed the bibliography.

Contents

Introduction

One form which distinctions commonly take is, "All things of **1** sort S are either F or G; nothing is both." S here represents a general class of entities (e.g., animals, propositions, illnesses) and F and G are properties which members of that class have. That is, some are F, and the others are G. Examples might be cold-blooded vs. warm-blooded animals, true vs. false propositions, chronic vs. temporary illness. Though there are of course many ways to divide up things of a given sort S according to whether or not they have some property, we usually speak of drawing a distinction when we mean to point out some non-obvious or perhaps unheeded difference between entities of some sort. There is no *general* purpose for doing this—that is, there is no *one* reason for drawing distinctions in general. Sometimes it is to correct or avoid actual or imminent confusion. Sometimes it is to facilitate discussion by dividing a question into several sub-questions. We shall see examples of both uses of distinction making.

For the form of distinction just outlined, then, we may say that to draw a distinction is to discern, note, or point out that things of sort S are of (at least) two kinds, frequently or commonly for the purpose of correcting or avoiding some confusion or mistake or dividing up an issue to facilitate discussion. An example of this form of distinction drawing occurs in David Hume's *A Treatise of Human Nature*.[1] Hume draws a distinction between ideas (things of sort S) which are simple (F) and those which are complex[2] (G), and on the very next page says

---

[1] David Hume, *A Treatise of Human Nature*, L. A. Selby-Bigge, ed., London: Oxford University Press, 1967 (1888).
[2] *Ibid.*, p. 2.

". . . I must make use of the distinction of perception into *simple* and *complex* . . . tho' there is in general a great resemblance betwixt our complex impressions and ideas, yet the rule is not universally true, that they are exact copies of each other. . . . We may next consider how the case stands with our *simple* perceptions. After the most accurate examination . . . I venture to affirm, that the rule holds without any exception. . . ."[3] Thus Hume, in answering the question of whether for every idea we have we once had a corresponding experience, says we must remember the distinction that was drawn (by him) between ideas (S) which are simple (F) and those which are complex (G) and ask the question of each one in turn. We see then that Hume sets out a distinction whose general form is "All things of sort S are either F or G" and then goes on to discuss each kind of S separately and to compare them with each other.

Distinction drawing, on the other hand, can follow a rather different form. This second form can be expressed in general terms as "The word (phrase) W can be understood to mean either M or N." Thus distinctions are commonly made between two (or more) senses or uses of a word or phrase, again not just for the sake of making distinctions but because some point depends on it. A classic example of this use of distinction-drawing occurs in William James' lecture on the nature of the philosophical school called Pragmatism.[4] James, in attempting to illustrate how the pragmatic method works, recounts a story in which a dispute occurs over the following puzzle: Suppose a squirrel is traversing the circumference of a tree and at the same time a man is walking around the tree. The squirrel manages to keep just on the other side of the tree, away from the man, the whole time. Now supposing they both make a full circle round the tree, has the man walked around the squirrel? Writes James, "Mindful of the scholastic adage that whenever you meet a contradiction you must make a distinction, I immediately sought and found one. . . ."[5] James goes on to point out that the man did go around the squirrel in the sense of going to the north, west, south, and east of him. But "around" also means to the left, rear, right, and front of him. Since the man and the squirrel maintained the same position relative to

---

[3] *Ibid.*, p. 3.
[4] William James, *Pragmatism: A New Name for Some Old Ways of Thinking*, Lecture II, New York: Longmans, Green, 1907, pp. 43–81.
[5] *Ibid.*, p. 44.

each other during their trip the man did not go around the squirrel in *that* sense. "Make the distinction, and there is no occasion for any further dispute."[6]

Quite clearly in this case the purpose of drawing the distinction is not to organize the discussion (as it was in Hume) but to correct an actual confusion.

There is a rather more striking difference between the two examples of distinctions we have considered; indeed, the difference is contained in the very words in which the form of the distinction was set out. For the first formulation spoke of *things* of a certain sort S whereas the second spoke of *words* with certain meanings. Are some distinctions, then, between *things* and others between *words?* Are distinctions between words or senses of words not about *things* at all? Herein we have the seeds of the complaint that philosophers are only worried about *words,* that they spend their time drawing distinctions and talking about meanings and senses and never get down to "the real issues." We of course have already acknowledged this much of the charge—that distinction drawing is not a valuable end-product of intellectual activity but is a means to some other goal. But in addition the complaint assumes something which is not strictly correct. It assumes that the subject matter of distinction drawing is indeed words rather than things. In the case of Hume, this was not even *prima facie* true. Hume was obviously not engaged in pointing out a difference in what is meant by the *words* "simple" and "complex." We all knew the difference between the meanings of the *words.* Rather, what Hume was concerned with was to distinguish between two kinds of *things* (in this case, two kinds of ideas)— those which are simple and those which are complex.

The complaint might appear to be more justified in the case of examples like James' squirrel puzzle. For here the claim is explicit that words are what are at issue. But even in this case the matter is not quite so simple as it might first appear. For could we not just as easily say that in distinguishing two different senses of the word "around," James was pointing out that there are two *ways* in which something can go around something else, two *kinds* of "going around." In discussing what it is to give a definition John Austin writes ". . . although we may sensibly ask 'Do we *ride* the word "elephant" or the animal?' and equally sensibly 'Do we *write* the word or the animal?' it is nonsense to ask 'Do we *define* the word or the animal?' For defining an elephant (supposing we ever do this) is a compendious description of an operation involving both word and animal. . . ."[7]

The same thing could be said about drawing a distinction, at least the second form of drawing a distinction (indeed this sort of distinction drawing can be viewed as a kind of defining). That is, it could be said that in drawing a distinction we are at once distinguishing between words and marking differences in the world. In any case, this is certainly what the people who first made use of the analytic-synthetic distinction took themselves to be doing. But as we shall see, some distinctions give more trouble than others, some are more clearly and consistently drawn than others, and some give rise to more problems than they help solve. What, then, is the analytic-synthetic distinction? What was the aim of drawing it, and how well has it served the progress of philosophy?

The Varieties of Truth

The analytic-synthetic distinction conforms to what I have called the first form of distinction making. That is, the general form of this distinction is "All things of sort S are either F or G." In this case we substitute "analytic" for F and "synthetic" for G. But now, what are the "things" which have one or the other of these properties; of what sort of things do we say that they are analytic or synthetic? I think the simplest way to answer this question is to say truths and falsehoods. Whatever sort of thing can be said to be true[8] or false (whether it be, e.g., a sentence, a statement, or a proposition), that thing can be said to be either analytic or synthetic. For the sake of consistency in our discussion, let us say that it is propositions which are true (and false) and we will indicate specimens of these propositions by placing a sentence which expresses a given proposition in boldface type.

Let us consider three such propositions:

---

[7] John Austin, "Truth," *Proceedings of the Aristotelian Society,* Supplementary Volume XXIV, 1950.

[8] There are actually many sorts of things which can be said to be true but which are not relevant to this discussion such as arrows which fly true (straight) or someone being true (faithful) to his lover. When we speak of e.g., "the great and lasting truths" we are speaking of certain sentences or statements or propositions. These things are said to be "true" or "false" in the sense of "true" that here concerns us.

A. **Automobiles contribute to air pollution.**
B. **If all apples have seeds, then if there is an apple in this room, it has seeds.**
C. **No grandmother is childless.**

Philosophers have been struck by the fact that although all of these propositions are true, there are many striking differences between them. First, there are differences in *why* they are true or in what makes them true. Second, there are differences in how we *know* they are true. Third, there are differences between them as to whether, though true right now, they might at another time be false. Fourth, they are different with respect to how *certain* we can be that they are true, how much chance there is that we might be wrong in believing they are true.

Of course, these differences are not unrelated to each other. Take for example the second and fourth points. How you know something determines how certain you are about it. For example, if you know that Jones started the fight because you *saw* him start it you are more certain that he started it than if you had heard about the fight from a friend of a person who saw it.

But now let us take a closer look at some of these differences as they apply to our sample propositions. We can say that A is true *because* automobile engines are constructed in a certain way and use a certain sort of fuel. This means that were certain features of the world to change, were someone, e.g., to develop an engine which could burn its fuel completely or give off, say, water as a byproduct, then A would no longer be true but would become false. Thus, in order to *know* A is true we have to know something about the world, e.g., that such an engine has not yet replaced all conventional engines. To be *certain* that A is true we have to be *certain*, e.g., that automobiles around the world have not undergone such a modification or been replaced by automobiles with such a new type of engine.

On the other hand, though we know that B is true also, we do not need to know anything about the world (specifically, apples) in order to know that this proposition is true. We need only rely on our reasoning to see that *if* all apples have seeds then if there is an apple in this room it has seeds too. We do not need to know *whether* any apple actually has seeds in order to know this. Hence (or perhaps "this is because") the truth or falsity of B does not depend on any feature of the world; it is equally true whether apples have seeds or not, or even whether there are apples or not. To know that B is true we need rely neither on our eyes nor on the reliability of stories carried by our friends; we thus can avoid with respect to B some of the *uncertainties* we may on occasion have about a proposition like A. Finally, though there is disagreement about whether B is *about* apples at all, it is generally agreed that what makes B true is not some fact about apples, but rather the *form* of the proposition. By this I mean that proposition B remains true regardless of whether we substitute, e.g., "orange" for "apple" or even "football" for "apple." It is just as true that *if* all footballs (or whatever else you choose) have seeds, then if there is one in this room it has seeds, as is the corresponding proposition about apples.

Turning to example C, we see that it is like B in many respects. Just as we do not need to investigate apples to know B is true, so too we do not need to consult the hospital records to see whether or not there are any childless grandmothers. One is a grandmother only if she has children who themselves have children. But then this already grants that all grandmothers *have* children and hence are not childless. But C is unlike B in that whereas B was true in virtue of its *form,* C is true in virtue of the meaning of the word "grandmother" (or the concept "grandmother" or by virtue of "what it is to be a grandmother"). For this reason, even the effects of radiation won't change the truth of C. We can see that C, like B, is true *for all time.*

Without saying any more by way of characterizing the distinction for the moment, let us say that propositions like A are *synthetic* and those like B or C are *analytic.*

It is easy to see why philosophers have felt it is so important to get clear on the differences between such propositions as A on the one hand and B and C on the other (and other propositions which we will have occasion to look at shortly). For philosophers since Plato have been concerned with (1) how we can provide justification for the propositions we wish to affirm; (2) what degree of certainty we are entitled to have with respect to the truth of various propositions; (3) what makes a true proposition true. We of course have already seen at least partial answers to these problems in comparing our propositions A, B, and C with each other. And indeed, if all the propositions which philosophers were concerned to examine could be neatly sorted into three groups (i.e., as being akin to either A or B or C) philosophers likely would have ceased laboring over these issues long ago. But, in fact, it was not such propositions as A, B, and C which caused so much difficulty for philosophers, but a rather different set of propositions which seem to resist the characterizations which we have given of A and B and C alike.

What, then, are these propositions which have given philosophers so much trouble and which have thus played such a prominent part in the history of philosophy? One such proposition is **every event has a cause.** This particular proposition has been a metaphysical cornerstone for a number of philosophical systems, and the philosophers who actually denied it are a mere handful.[9] But now with which of our sample propositions should we class it? For on the one hand though the "world" seems to confirm its truth, we are prepared to accept no counterinstances. I mean by this that if we *should* wake up one morning and find that all automobiles had been fitted with a new type of engine which gave off only water as exhaust, that would make us change our tune, and we would have to then allow that automobiles do not contribute to air pollution. But would we ever be willing to accept someone's claim to have found an event with no cause? Or wouldn't we rather insist (after all, we are not superstitious) "There has to be an explanation—something must have caused it to happen." Notice we insist not just that there *is* an explanation, but that there *has* to be. In other words, we are saying that regardless of the way it may *look,* nothing anyone shows us will overthrow the proposition that every event (and hence this one) has a cause.

And yet this proposition, **every event has a cause,** seems not to be like B or C either. It is not, like B, true because of its form, nor does there seem to be anything in the meaning of the term "event" from which it would follow that every event has a cause. If the proposition were instead **every *effect* has a cause** then perhaps this could be said to be like **no grandmother is childless.** For to call something an effect is to say it is the effect *of* something; and to say that something is the effect of something else is just to say that "something else" caused it. But events are not events *of* anything, and so the proposition *every event has a cause* cannot be seen as being like C.

There are a host of other propositions which seem to resist being assimilated to A, B, or C and which for that reason, and

---

[9] Many, however, did exclude human action from its scope, thus disconnecting the "will" from the chain of causes.

because of their own intrinsic importance, have caused philosophers to pay a great deal of attention to the analytic-synthetic distinction as well as to a set of related distinctions.[10] Such propositions are: **no object can be in two places at the same time; no object can be red and green all over at the same time; all things being equal, one ought to keep his promises; no human being has the right to own another human being;** and finally, mathematical propositions such as **7 + 5 = 12.** A moment's reflection should show that these propositions, like **every event has a cause,** cannot easily be assimilated to our samples A or B or C.

Philosophy has recently added a unique strand to the tangle of issues surrounding the analytic-synthetic distinction by raising the question of whether such a distinction can even be made out (Quine) or at least whether it might be less misleading to leave it unmade (Austin). Whether they are ultimately correct, this in no way diminishes the importance of the distinction to the history of philosophy or the importance of the issues which gave rise to the distinction. It is likely that the distinction will survive and permeate philosophical discussion for a long time to come; it is a certainty that the issues which gave rise to the distinction will-persist as long as philosophy is being done.

[10] These other distinctions are a priori-a posteriori, necessary-contingent, conceptual-factual, logical-empirical. Except as these distinctions appear in the selections in this volume, no attempt will be made to characterize the relationships between them. To try to do so at this point might encourage the reader to try to understand a rather complicated schema without understanding how the various distinctions fit into the discussions out of which they arose. After acquainting himself with the writings in this volume, the reader may then wish to attempt to formulate how the distinctions are related to each other—he will soon see what a difficult and complicated matter it is.

Several recent writings contain sketches of the various ways in which these distinctions can be and have been made out, and these should prove helpful.

1. Jaakko Hintikka, "Are Logical Truths Analytic?" *Philosophical Review,* LXXIV, 2 (April 1965), 178–203.

2. J. M. E. Moravcsik, "The Analytic and the Nonempirical," *Journal of Philosophy,* LXII, 16 (August 1965), 415–429.

3. Wilfrid Sellars, "Is There a Synthetic *A Priori?" Philosophy of Science,* XX, 2 (1953), 121–138.

4. L. W. Sumner and John Woods, eds., *Necessary Truth: A Book of Readings,* New York: Random, 1969, pp. 3–9.

Gottfried Wilhelm von Leibniz (1646–1716)

First Truths

As was mentioned in the Introduction, the analytic-synthetic **9** distinction is just one of a group of distinctions, and one cannot adequately discuss any of them in historical perspective by itself. The other distinctions are a priori-a posteriori, necessary-contingent, conceptual-factual, and logical-empirical. Having said this much, however, it is extremely difficult to say more by way of characterizing these distinctions. To do so is to immediately involve oneself in philosophical positions with regard to substantive issues. The question is further hampered by the fact that there is no such thing as "the accepted definition" of the distinctions. As we proceed to compare the views of Leibniz with those of Hobbes and those of Hobbes with Kant's we will see examples of both kinds of difficulty.

Leibniz says of both necessary and contingent truths that "the concept of the predicate is in some way contained in the concept of the subject."[1] This notion is of course not entirely unfamiliar to us. We said in the previous section that **no grandmother is childless** is true in virtue of the very concept of what it is to be a grandmother, that the concept of a grandmother contains or includes a notion of having a child. But we of course wanted to limit this to propositions like C, whereas on Leibniz's account all true propositions are in this respect like C (it is important to note, though, that this is a claim about both necessary and contingent truths, not a definition of them).

From Gottfried Wilhelm Leibniz—Philosophical Papers and Letters, L. E. Loemker, ed., pp. 267–279. Dordrecht: D. Reidel Publishing Company, 1969. © in The Netherlands by D. Reidel Publishing Company, Dordrecht. Reprinted by permission of the publisher.

[1] Gottfried Wilhelm von Leibniz, "Necessary and Contingent Truths," in T. V. Smith and Marjorie Grene, eds., From Descartes to Kant, Chicago: University of Chicago Press, 1940, p. 346.

First truths are those which predicate something of itself or deny the opposite of its opposite. For example, *A* is *A,* or *A* is not non-*A;* if it is true that *A* is *B,* it is false that *A* is not *B* or that *A* is non-*B.* Likewise, everything is what it is; everything is similar or equal to itself; nothing is greater or less than itself. These and other truths of this kind, though they may have various degrees of priority, can nevertheless all be grouped under the one name of *identities.*

All other truths are reduced to first truths with the aid of definitions or by the analysis of concepts; in this consists *proof* a priori, which is independent of experience. I shall give as example this proposition which is accepted as an axiom by mathematicians and all other people alike: the whole is greater than its part, or the part is less than the whole. This is very easily demonstrated from the definition of less or greater, with the addition of a primitive axiom or identity. For that is *less* which is equal to a part of another thing (the *greater*). This definition is very easily understood and is consistent with the general practice of men, when they compare things with each other and measure the excess by subtracting an amount equal to the smaller from the greater. Hence one may reason as follows. A part is equal to the whole (namely, to itself, by the axiom of identity, according to which each thing is equal to itself). But what is equal to a part of a whole is less than the whole (by the definition of less). Therefore the part is less than the whole.

The predicate or consequent therefore always inheres in the subject or antecedent. And as Aristotle, too, observed, the nature of truth in general or the connection between the terms of a proposition consists in this fact. In identities this connection and the inclusion of the predicate in the subject are explicit; in all other propositions they are implied and must be revealed through the analysis of the concepts, which constitutes a demonstration a priori.

This is true, moreover, in every affirmative truth, universal or singular, necessary or contingent, whether its terms are intrinsic or extrinsic denominations. Here lies hidden a wonderful secret which contains the nature of contingency or the essential distinction between necessary and contingent truths and which removes the difficulty involved in a fatal necessity determining even free things.

These matters have not been adequately considered because they are too easy, but there follow from them many things of great importance. At once they give rise to the accepted axiom that *there is nothing without a reason, or no effect without a cause.* Otherwise there would be truth which could not be proved a priori or resolved into identities—contrary to the nature of truth, which is always either expressly or implicitly identical. It follows also that, if there is a correspondence between two data in a determining series, then there will also be a correspondence of the same kind in the series sought for and determined by the former. For no difference can be accounted for unless its reason is found in the data. A corollary, or, better, an example, of this is the postulate of Archimedes stated at the beginning of his book on the balance—that if the arms of a balance and its weights are supposed equal, everything will be in equilibrium. This also gives a *reason for eternal things.* If it be assumed that the world has existed from eternity and has contained only spheres, a reason should have to be given why it contains spheres rather than cubes.

It follows also that *there are no two individual things in nature which differ only numerically.* For surely it must be possible to give a reason why they are different, and this must be sought in some differences within themselves. Thus the observation of Thomas Aquinas about separate intelligences, which he declared never differ in number alone, must be applied to other things also. Never are two eggs, two leaves, or two blades of grass in a garden to be found exactly similar to each other. So perfect similarity occurs only in incomplete and abstract concepts, where matters are conceived, not in their totality but according to a certain single viewpoint, as when we consider only figures and neglect the figured matter. So geometry is right in studying similar triangles, even though two perfectly similar material triangles are never found. And, although gold or some other metal, or salt, and many liquids, may be taken for homogeneous bodies, this can be admitted only as concerns the senses and not as if it were true in an exact sense.

It follows further that *there are no purely extrinsic denominations* which have no basis at all in the denominated thing itself. For the concept of the denominated subject necessarily involves the concept of the predicate. Likewise, whenever the denomination of a thing is changed, some variation has to occur in the thing itself.

The complete or perfect concept of an individual substance involves all its predicates, past, present, and future. For certainly it is already true now that a future predicate will be a predicate in the future, and so it is contained in the concept of the thing. Therefore there is contained in the perfect individual concepts of Peter or Judas, considered as merely possible concepts and setting aside the divine decree to create them, everything that will happen to them, whether necessarily or freely. And all this is known by God. Thus it is obvious that God elects from an infinity of possible individuals those whom he judges best suited to the supreme and secret ends of his wisdom. In an exact sense, he does not decree that Peter should sin or Judas be damned but only that, in preference to other possible individuals, Peter, who will sin—certainly, indeed, yet not necessarily but freely—and Judas, who will suffer damnation—under the same condition—shall come into existence, or that the possible concept shall become actual. And although the eternal possible concept of Peter also contains his future salvation, the cooperation of grace is not yet absent from it, for this same perfect concept of this possible Peter also contains as a possibility the help of divine grace which will be granted to him. . . .

Gottfried Wilhelm von Leibniz (1646–1716)

Necessary and Contingent Truths

A true affirmation is one, the predicate of which is present in **13** the subject. Thus in every true affirmative proposition, necessary or contingent, universal or singular, the concept of the predicate is in some way contained in the concept of the subject, so that he who perfectly understood each concept as GOD understands it, would by that very fact perceive that the predicate is present in the subject. Hence it follows that all the knowledge of propositions which is in GOD, whether it be of simple understanding about the essences of things, or of vision about the existences of things, or mediate knowledge about conditioned existences, results immediately from the perfect intellection of each term, which can be subject or predicate of any proposition; or that the a priori knowledge of complex things springs from the understanding of those that are incomplex.

An absolutely necessary proposition is one which can be resolved into identical propositions, or the opposite of which implies a contradiction! Let me show this by an example in numbers. I shall call binary every number which can be exactly divided by two, and ternary or quaternary—every one that can be exactly divided by three or four, and so on. For we understand every number to be resolved into those which exactly divide it. I say therefore that this proposition: that a duodenary number is quaternary, is absolutely necessary, since it can be resolved into identical propositions in the following way. A duodenary number is binary-senary (by definition); senary is binary ternary (by definition). Therefore a

From *From Descartes to Kant,* T. V. Smith and Marjorie Grene, eds., Part II, Chapter VI, pp. 346–352. Chicago: University of Chicago Press, 1940. Copyright © 1940 by the University of Chicago. Reprinted by permission of the University of Chicago Press.

duodenary number is binary binary ternary. Further binary binary is quaternary (by definition). Therefore a duodenary number is quaternary ternary. Therefore a duodenary number is quaternary. Q.E.D. But even if other definitions had been given, it could always have been shown that it comes to the same thing. Therefore I call this necessity metaphysical or geometrical. What lacks such necessity, I call contingent; but what implies a contradiction, or that the opposite of which is necessary, is called *impossible*. Other things are called *possible*. In contingent truth, even though the predicate is really present in the subject, nevertheless by whatever resolution you please of either term, indefinitely continued, you will never arrive at demonstration or identity. And it is for GOD alone, comprehending the infinite all at once, to perceive how one is present in the other, and to understand a priori the perfect reason of contingency, which in creatures is furnished (a *posteriori*) by experience. Thus contingent truths are related to necessary as surd roots, i.e. the roots of incommensurable numbers, to the expressible roots of commensurable numbers. For just as it can be shown that a small number is present in another greater number, by reducing both to the greatest common measure, so too essential propositions or truths are demonstrated: i.e., a resolution is carried on until it arrives at terms which it is established by the definitions are common to either term. But as a greater number contains a certain other incommensurable number, and let whatever resolution you please be continued to infinity, it never arrives at a common measure—so in contingent truth, it never arrives at demonstration however much you may resolve the concepts. There is only this difference, that in surd roots we can nevertheless carry out demonstrations, by showing that the error is less than any assignable number, but in contingent truths not even this is conceded to a created mind. And so I consider that I have unfolded something secret, which has long perplexed even myself—while I did not understand how the predicate could be in the subject, and yet the proposition not be necessary. But the knowledge of things geometrical and the analysis of infinities kindled this light for me, so that I understood that concepts too are resoluble to infinity.

Hence we now learn that propositions which pertain to the essences and those which pertain to the existences of things are different. Essential surely are those which can be demonstrated from the resolution of terms, that is, which are necessary, or virtually identical, and the opposite of which, moreover, are impossible or virtually contradictory. And these are the eternal truths. They did not obtain only while the world existed, but they would also obtain if GOD had created a world with a different plan. But from these, existential or contingent truths differ entirely. Their truth is understood a priori by the infinite mind alone, and they cannot be demonstrated by any resolution. They are of the sort that are true at a certain time, and they do not only express what pertains to the possibility of things, but also what actually does exist, or would exist contingently if certain things were supposed. For example, take the proposition, I am now living, the sun is shining. For suppose I say that the sun is shining in our hemisphere at this hour, because up to now its motion has been such that, granted its continuation, this certainly follows. Even then (not to mention the non-necessary obligation of its continuing) that its motion even before this was so much and of this kind is similarly a contingent truth, for which again the reason should be inquired—nor could it be fully produced except from the perfect knowledge of all parts of the universe. This, however, exceeds all created powers. For there is no portion of matter, which is not actually subdivided into other parts; hence the parts of any body whatsoever are actually infinite. Thus neither the sun nor any other body can be perfectly known by a creature. Much less can we arrive at the end of the analysis if we search for the mover causing the motion of any body whatsoever and again for the mover of this; for we shall always arrive at smaller bodies without end. But GOD is not in need of that transition from one contingent to another earlier or simpler contingent,— a transition which can never have an end (as also one contingent is in fact not the cause of another, even though it may seem so to us). But he perceives in any individual substance from its very concept the truth of all its accidents, calling in nothing extrinsic, since any one at all involves in its way all the others and the whole universe. Hence into all propositions into which existence and time enter, by that very fact the whole series of things enters, nor can the now or here be understood except in relation to other things. For this reason such propositions do not allow of a demonstration or terminable resolution by which their truth might appear. And the same holds of all accidents of individual created substances. Indeed even though some one were able to know the whole series of the universe, he still could not state the reason of it, except by having undertaken the comparison of it with all other possible universes. From this it is clear why a demonstration of no contingent proposition can be found, however far the resolution of concepts be continued.

It must not be thought, however, that only singular propositions are contingent, for there are (and can be inferred by induction) some propositions true for the most part; and there are also propositions almost always true at least naturally, so that an exception is ascribed to a miracle. Indeed, I think there are certain propositions most universally true in this series of things, and certainly never to be violated even by miracle, not that they could not be violated by GOD, but that when he himself chose this series of things, by that very fact he decided to observe them (as the specific properties of this very series chosen). And through these propositions set up once for all by the force of the divine decree, it is possible to state the reason for other universal propositions and also for many contingent propositions which can be observed in this universe. For from the first essential laws of the series, true without exception, which contain the whole aim of GOD in choosing the universe, and even include miracles as well, subaltern laws of nature can be derived, which have only physical necessity, and which are not modified except by miracle, by reason of an intuition of some more powerful final cause. And from these finally are inferred others the universality of which is still less; and GOD can also reveal to creatures this kind of demonstration of intermediate universals from one another, a part of which makes up physical science. But one could never by any analysis come to the most universal laws nor to the perfect reasons for individual things; for this knowledge is necessarily appropriate only to GOD. Nor indeed should it disturb any one, that I have said there are certain laws essential to this series of things, since we have nevertheless said above that these very laws are not necessary and essential, but contingent and existential. For since the fact that the series itself exists is contingent, and depends on a free decree of GOD, its laws too, considered absolutely, will be contingent; hypothetically, however, if the series is supposed, they are necessary and so far essential.

These things will now be of advantage to us in distinguishing free substances from others. The accidents of every individual substance if they are predicated of it constitute a contingent proposition, which does not have metaphysical necessity. And the fact that this stone tends downward when its support is removed, is not a necessary but a contingent proposition; nor can such an event be demonstrated from the concept of this stone with the help of the universal concepts which enter into it; and so GOD alone perceives this perfectly. For he alone knows, whether he himself is not going to suspend by a miracle that subaltern law of nature by which heavy things are driven downward. Nor do others understand the most universal laws, nor can they go through the infinite analysis which is necessary to connect the concept of this stone with the concept of the whole universe or with the most universal laws. However, this at least can be foreknown from the subaltern laws of nature, that unless the law of gravity is suspended by a miracle, descent follows. But free or intelligent substances have in fact something greater and more marvellous in the direction of a certain imitation of GOD; so that they are bound by no definite subaltern laws of nature, but (as if it were a privation by a certain miracle), they act from the spontaneity of their own power alone, and by an intuition of some final cause they break the nexus and course of efficient causes according to their will. And so true is this, that there is no creature knowing of hearts, who could predict with certainty what another mind will choose according to the laws of nature,—as it can be predicted in another case, at least by an angel, how some body will act if the course of nature be not interrupted. For as the course of the universe is changed by the free will of GOD, so by the free will of the mind the course of its thoughts is changed; so that no subaltern universal laws sufficient for predicting their choice can be found in minds as they are in bodies. This does not, however, at all prevent the future actions of the mind, like his own future actions, from being fixed for GOD, as they are also fixed for the series of things which he chooses. And surely he knows perfectly the strength of his own decree, and also understands at the same time what is contained in the concept of this mind which he himself has admitted into the number of things that are to exist—in so much as it involves this very series of things and its most universal laws. And although this one thing is most true, that the mind never chooses what now appears worse, still it does not always choose what now appears better; since it can put off and suspend judgment till further deliberation and turn its attention to thinking of other things. As to the question whether this will be done, it is not sufficiently determined by any evidence or definite law; certainly not in those minds, which are not sufficiently confirmed in good or evil. For in the case of the blessed another statement must be made.

Hence also it can be understood, what that indifference is which attends liberty. Surely as contingency is opposed to metaphysical necessity, so indifference excludes not only metaphysical, but also physical necessity. It is, in a way, a matter of physical necessity, that GOD should do all things as well as possible (although it is not in the power of any creature to apply this universal rule to individuals, and thus to draw any certain consequences from the divine free actions). It is also a matter of physical necessity that those confirmed in good, angels or blessed, should act from virtue (in such a way, in fact, that it can be predicted with certainty even by a creature, how they will act). It is a matter of physical necessity, that what is heavy strives downward, that the angles of incidence and of reflection are equal, and other things of that kind. But it is not a matter of physical necessity that men should in this life choose some particular good, howsoever specious and apparent it may be, although that is sometimes emphatically to be presumed. For although it may never be possible for that complete metaphysical indifference to exist, such that the mind should be disposed in quite the same way to either one of two contradictories and, again, that anything should be in equilibrium, as it were, with all its nature, (for we have already observed that even a future predicate is really already present in the concept of the subject, and that therefore mind is not, metaphysically speaking, indifferent, since GOD from the perfect concept of it which he has already perceives all its future accidents, and since mind is not now indifferent to its everlasting concept), still the physical indifference of mind is great enough so that it is certainly not under physical necessity (nor yet metaphysical, i.e., so that no universal reason or law of nature is assignable from which any Creature, however perfect and learned in the state of this mind, can infer with certainty, what the mind, at least naturally (without the extraordinary concourse of GOD), will choose. . . .

Thomas Hobbes
(1588–1679)

Of Proposition

Hobbes in defining necessary truth writes, "A necessary propo- **19**
sition is when nothing can at any time be conceived or feigned,
whereof the subject is the name, but the predicate also is the
name of the same thing . . . But in a contingent *proposition*
. . . though this were true, every man is a liar, yet because the
word liar *is no part of a compounded name equivalent to the*
name man, *that proposition is called not necessary but con-*
tingent, . . ."[1] *But now, since Leibniz claims that in all true*
propositions the concept of the predicate is contained in the
concept of the subject, there could on his account be no
contingent propositions in the sense in which this expression
is defined by Hobbes.[2] *For if Leibniz were correct and the con-*
cept of the predicate were contained in the concept of the
subject in all true propositions then for all true propositions
"nothing can at any time be conceived or feigned, whereof the
subject is the name but the predicate also is the name of the
same thing." But this is just Hobbes' definition of necessary
truth and hence all propositions would turn out to be necessary.
This result was not at all what Leibniz intended and of course
shows no flaw in his thinking. It merely shows that one cannot
assume that because one sees the same term in reading two
philosophers (in this case the term "necessary") that one is
dealing with the same concept.

From *Hobbes—English Works,* William Molesworth, ed., pp. 37–38. London:
John Bohn, 1839.

[1] Thomas Hobbes, "Concerning Body," in William Molesworth, ed., *English
Works,* Vol. I, London: John Bohn, 1839, p. 38.

[2] In addition to the discussion contained in this volume, Leibniz addresses
the problem of how there could be contingent truths in "On Freedom," in
Leroy Loemker, ed., *Philosophical Papers and Letters,* Dordrecht: D. Reidel
Publishing Co., 1969.

Fifthly, propositions are distinguished into *necessary,* that is, necessarily true; and true, but not necessarily, which they call *contingent.* A *necessary* proposition is when nothing can at any time be conceived or feigned, whereof the subject is the name, but the predicate also is the name of the same thing; as *man is a living creature* is a necessary proposition, because at what time soever we suppose the name *man* agrees with any thing, at that time the name *living-creature* also agrees with the same. But a *contingent* proposition is that, which at one time may be true, at another time false; as *every crow is black;* which may perhaps be true now, but false hereafter. Again, in every *necessary* proposition, the predicate is either equivalent to the subject, as in this, *man is a rational living creature;* or part of an equivalent name, as in this, *man is a living creature,* for the name *rational-living-creature,* or *man,* is compounded of these two, *rational* and *living-creature.* But in a *contingent* proposition this cannot be; for though this were true, *every man is a liar,* yet because the word *liar* is no part of a compounded name equivalent to the name *man,* that proposition is not to be called *necessary,* but *contingent,* though it should happen to be true always. And therefore those propositions only are *necessary,* which are of sempiternal truth, that is, true at all times. From hence also it is manifest, that truth adheres not to things, but to speech only, for some truths are eternal; for it will be eternally true, *if man, then living-creature;* but that any *man,* or *living-creature,* should exist eternally, is not necessary.

Immanuel Kant (1724–1804)

Introduction to the Critique of Pure Reason

Kant writes ". . . if we have a proposition which in being **21** thought is thought as necessary, it is an a priori judgment."[1] A priori judgments are generally understood to be those capable of being known to be true (or false) independent of experience, as are our examples B and C in the Introduction. But according to Kant not all a priori judgments are such that either the concept of the predicate is contained in the concept of the subject or else true in virtue of its form. Thus there are for Kant necessary (and hence a priori) truths which nevertheless are not true in virtue of the concept of the predicate being contained in the concept of the subject or in virtue of the form. (These propositions include all the "problem" propositions we noted in the last part of the Introduction.) This being the case, neither Kant's notion of "necessary" nor Kant's notion of "a priori" coincides precisely with Hobbes' notion of "necessary." Kant, however, does make a different distinction which at first glance looks as though it might coincide with Hobbes's distinction between necessary and contingent truths. That is, the distinction between "analytic" and "synthetic" truths, and it is the distinction between truths whose predicate is "contained" in the subject and those where this is not the case. It might now seem that there is just a difference in labels between Hobbes and Kant—that Hobbes's distinction between necessary and contingent is really Kant's distinction between analytic and synthetic truth. But unfortunately the matter is not as simple as

From *Immanuel Kant's Critique of Pure Reason*, Norman Kemp Smith, trans., pp. 41–55. New York: St. Martin's Press, 1929. Reprinted by permission of St. Martin's Press, Inc., Macmillan and Co. Ltd., London and the Macmillan Co. of Canada, Ltd.

[1] Immanuel Kant, *Critique of Pure Reason* (*1781*), Norman Kemp Smith, trans., New York: St. Martin's, 1961, p. 43.

that, for Hobbes writes, "but a contingent proposition is that which at one time may be true and another time false; as **every crow is black;** *which may perhaps be true now, but false hereafter."*[2] *But for Kant, not all synthetic propositions can be at one time true and at another false. There are synthetic a priori truths (one example allegedly being* **every event has a cause;** *which, while not true in virtue of the relation of the concepts (or meanings) involved, nevertheless are not capable of being true for one period of time and false for another. Thus "contingent" as defined by Hobbes is not equivalent to Kant's notion of "synthetic." Hobbes did define necessity in such a way that he means by this what Kant means by analytic; but in the other half of the distinction there is a divergence. The consequence of this is rather striking. Since both men, in drawing their respective distinctions, were dividing all entities of a certain sort (in this case, "truths") exclusively and exhaustively into two groups, their distinctions are literally incompatible with each other. Some truths are analytic (Kant)/ necessary (Hobbes); these terms are equivalent. The rest are synthetic (Kant)/contingent (Hobbes). But since "synthetic" does not mean "contingent" those two classes contain different members while at the same time having to include the same members (to wit, all propositions which are not analytic/ necessary). Therefore one of the distinctions must be abandoned, though it is not at all obvious which. For this issue is really the very issue of whether there are synthetic a priori truths, truths which are necessary yet which are not simply a function of the relationship between our concepts.*

I. The Distinction Between Pure and Empirical Knowledge

There can be no doubt that all our knowledge begins with experience. For how should our faculty of knowledge be awakened into action did not objects affecting our senses partly of themselves produce representations, partly arouse the activity of our understanding to compare these representations, and, by combining or separating them, work up the raw material of the sensible impressions into that knowledge of

---

[2] Thomas Hobbes, *Concerning Body*, in William Molesworth, ed. and trans., *English Works*, Vol I, London: John Bohn, 1839, p. 38.

objects which is entitled experience? In the order of time, therefore, we have no knowledge antecedent to experience, and with experience all our knowledge begins.

But though all our knowledge begins with experience, it does not follow that it all arises out of experience. For it may well be that even our empirical knowledge is made up of what we receive through impressions and of what our own faculty of knowledge (sensible impressions serving merely as the occasion) supplies from itself. If our faculty of knowledge makes any such addition, it may be that we are not in a position to distinguish it from the raw material, until with long practice of attention we have become skilled in separating it.

This, then, is a question which at least calls for closer examination, and does not allow of any off-hand answer:— whether there is any knowledge that is thus independent of experience and even of all impressions of the senses. Such knowledge is entitled *a priori,* and distinguished from the *empirical,* which has its sources *a posteriori,* that is, in experience.

The expression '*a priori*' does not, however, indicate with sufficient precision the full meaning of our question. For it has been customary to say, even of much knowledge that is derived from empirical sources, that we have it or are capable of having it *a priori,* meaning thereby that we do not derive it immediately from experience, but from a universal rule—a rule which is itself, however, borrowed by us from experience. Thus we would say of a man who undermined the foundations of his house, that he might have known *a priori* that it would fall, that is, that he need not have waited for the experience of its actually falling. But still he could not know this completely *a priori.* For he had first to learn through experience that bodies are heavy, and therefore fall when their supports are withdrawn.

In what follows, therefore, we shall understand by *a priori* knowledge, not knowledge independent of this or that experience, but knowledge absolutely independent of all experience. Opposed to it is empirical knowledge, which is knowledge possible only *a posteriori,* that is, through experience. *A priori* modes of knowledge are entitled pure when there is no admixture of anything empirical. Thus, for instance, the proposition, 'every alteration has its cause', while an *a priori* proposition, is not a pure proposition, because alteration is a concept which can be derived only from experience.

II. We Are in Possession of Certain Modes of *A Priori* Knowledge, and Even the Common Understanding is Never Without Them

What we here require is a criterion by which to distinguish with certainty between pure and empirical knowledge. Experience teaches us that a thing is so and so, but not that it cannot be otherwise. First, then, if we have a proposition which in being thought is thought as *necessary,* it is an a *priori* judgment; and if, besides, it is not derived from any proposition except one which also has the validity of a necessary judgment, it is an absolutely a *priori* judgment. Secondly, experience never confers on its judgments true or strict, but only assumed and comparative *universality,* through induction. We can properly only say, therefore, that, so far as we have hitherto observed, there is no exception to this or that rule. If, then, a judgment is thought with strict universality, that is, in such manner that no exception is allowed as possible, it is not derived from experience, but is valid absolutely a *priori.* Empirical universality is only an arbitrary extension of a validity holding in most cases to one which holds in all, for instance, in the proposition, 'all bodies are heavy'. When, on the other hand, strict universality is essential to a judgment, this indicates a special source of knowledge, namely, a faculty of a *priori* knowledge. Necessity and strict universality are thus sure criteria of a *priori* knowledge, and are inseparable from one another. But since in the employment of these criteria the contingency of judgments is sometimes more easily shown than their empirical limitation, or, as sometimes also happens, their unlimited universality can be more convincingly proved than their necessity, it is advisable to use the two criteria separately, each by itself being infallible.

Now it is easy to show that there actually are in human knowledge judgments which are necessary and in the strictest sense universal, and which are therefore pure a *priori* judgments. If an example from the sciences be desired, we have only to look to any of the propositions of mathematics; if we seek an example from the understanding in its quite ordinary employment, the proposition, 'every alteration must have a cause', will serve our purpose. In the latter case, indeed, the very concept of a cause so manifestly contains the concept of a necessity of connection with an effect and of the strict universality of the rule, that the concept would be altogether lost if we attempted to derive it, as Hume has done, from a repeated association of that which happens with that which precedes, and from a custom of connecting representations, a custom originating in this repeated association, and constituting therefore a merely subjective necessity. Even without appealing to such examples, it is possible to show that pure *a priori* principles are indispensable for the possibility of experience, and so to prove their existence *a priori*. For whence could experience derive its certainty, if all the rules, according to which it proceeds, were always themselves empirical, and therefore contingent? Such rules could hardly be regarded as first principles. At present, however, we may be content to have established the fact that our faculty of knowledge does have a pure employment, and to have shown what are the criteria of such an employment.

Such a *priori* origin is manifest in certain concepts, no less than in judgments. If we remove from our empirical concept of a body, one by one, every feature in it which is [merely] empirical, the colour, the hardness or softness, the weight, even the impenetrability, there still remains the space which the body (now entirely vanished) occupied, and this cannot be removed. Again, if we remove from our empirical concept of any object, corporeal or incorporeal, all properties which experience has taught us, we yet cannot take away that property through which the object is thought as substance or as inhering in a substance (although this concept of substance is more determinate than that of an object in general). Owing, therefore, to the necessity with which this concept of substance forces itself upon us, we have no option save to admit that it has its seat in our faculty of *a priori* knowledge.

III. Philosophy Stands in Need of a Science Which Shall Determine the Possibility, the Principles, and the Extent of all *A Priori* Knowledge

But what is still more extraordinary than all the preceding is this, that certain modes of knowledge leave the field of all possible experiences and have the appearance of extending the scope of our judgments beyond all limits of experience, and this by means of concepts to which no corresponding object can ever be given in experience.

It is precisely by means of the latter modes of knowledge, in a realm beyond the world of the senses, where experience can yield neither guidance nor correction, that our reason carries on those enquiries which owing to their importance we consider to be far more excellent, and in their purpose far more lofty, than all that the understanding can learn in the field of appearances. Indeed we prefer to run every risk of error rather than desist from such urgent enquiries, on the ground of their dubious character, or from disdain and indifference. These unavoidable problems set by pure reason itself are *God, freedom,* and *immortality.* The science which, with all its preparations, is in its final intention directed solely to their solution is metaphysics; and its procedure is at first dogmatic, that is, it confidently sets itself to this task without any previous examination of the capacity or incapacity of reason for so great an undertaking.

Now it does indeed seem natural that, as soon as we have left the ground of experience, we should, through careful enquiries, assure ourselves as to the foundations of any building that we propose to erect, not making use of any knowledge that we possess without first determining whence it has come, and not trusting to principles without knowing their origin. It is natural, that is to say, that the question should first be considered, how the understanding can arrive at all this knowledge *a priori,* and what extent, validity, and worth it may have. Nothing, indeed, could be more natural, if by the term 'natural' we signify what fittingly and reasonably ought to happen. But if we mean by 'natural' what ordinarily happens, then on the contrary nothing is more natural and more intelligible than the fact that this enquiry has been so long neglected. For one part of this knowledge, the mathematical, has long been of established reliability, and so gives rise to a favourable presumption as regards the other part, which may yet be of quite different nature. Besides, once we are outside the circle of experience, we can be sure of not being *contradicted* by experience. The charm of extending our knowledge is so great that nothing short of encountering a direct contradiction can suffice to arrest us in our course; and this can be avoided, if we are careful in our fabrications—which none the less will still remain fabrications. Mathematics gives us a shining example of how far, independently of experience, we can progress in *a priori* knowledge. It does, indeed, occupy itself with objects and with knowledge solely in so far as they allow of being exhibited in intuition. But this circumstance is easily overlooked, since this intuition can itself be given a *priori*, and is therefore hardly to be distinguished from a bare and pure concept. Misled by such a proof of the power of reason, the demand for the extension of knowledge recognises no limits. The light dove, cleaving the air in her free flight, and feeling its resistance, might imagine that its flight would be still easier in empty space. It was thus that Plato left the world of the senses, as setting too narrow limits to the understanding, and ventured out beyond it on the wings of the ideas, in the empty space of the pure understanding. He did not observe that with all his efforts he made no advance—meeting no resistance that might, as it were, serve as a support upon which he could take a stand, to which he could apply his powers, and so set his understanding in motion. It is, indeed, the common fate of human reason to complete its speculative structures as speedily as may be, and only afterwards to enquire whether the foundations are reliable. All sorts of excuses will then be appealed to, in order to reassure us of their solidity, or rather indeed to enable us to dispense altogether with so late and so dangerous an enquiry. But what keeps us, during the actual building, free from all apprehension and suspicion, and flatters us with a seeming thoroughness, is this other circumstance, namely, that a great, perhaps the greatest, part of the business of our reason consists in analysis of the concepts which we already have of objects. This analysis supplies us with a considerable body of knowledge, which, while nothing but explanation or elucidation of what has already been thought in our concepts, though in a confused manner, is yet prized as being, at least as regards its form, new insight. But so far as the matter or content is concerned, there has been no extension of our previously possessed concepts, but only an analysis of them. Since this procedure yields real knowledge a *priori*, which progresses in an assured and useful fashion, reason is so far misled as surreptitiously to introduce, without itself being aware of so doing, assertions of an entirely different order, in which it attaches to given concepts others completely foreign to them, and moreover attaches them a *priori*. And yet it is not known how reason can be in position to do this. Such a question is never so much as thought of. I shall therefore at once proceed to deal with the difference between these two kinds of knowledge.

In all judgments in which the relation of a subject to the predicate is thought (I take into consideration affirmative judgments only, the subsequent application to negative judgments being easily made), this relation is possible in two different ways. Either the predicate B belongs to the subject A, as something which is (covertly) contained in this concept A; or B lies outside the concept A, although it does indeed stand in connection with it. In the one case I entitle the judgment analytic, in the other synthetic. Analytic judgments (affirmative) are therefore those in which the connection of the predicate with the subject is thought through identity; those in which this connection is thought without identity should be entitled synthetic. The former, as adding nothing through the predicate to the concept of the subject, but merely breaking it up into those constituent concepts that have all along been thought in it, although confusedly, can also be entitled explicative. The latter, on the other hand, add to the concept of the subject a predicate which has not been in any wise thought in it, and which no analysis could possibly extract from it; and they may therefore be entitled ampliative. If I say, for instance, 'All bodies are extended', this is an analytic judgment. For I do not require to go beyond the concept which I connect with 'body' in order to find extension as bound up with it. To meet with this predicate, I have merely to analyse the concept, that is, to become conscious to myself of the manifold which I always think in that concept. The judgment is therefore analytic. But when I say, 'All bodies are heavy', the predicate is something quite different from anything that I think in the mere concept of body in general; and the addition of such a predicate therefore yields a synthetic judgment.

Judgments of experience, as such, are one and all synthetic. For it would be absurd to found an analytic judgment on experience. Since, in framing the judgment, I must not go outside my concept, there is no need to appeal to the testimony of experience in its support. That a body is extended is a proposition that holds *a priori* and is not empirical. For, before appealing to experience, I have already in the concept of body all the conditions required for my judgment. I have only to extract from it, in accordance with the principle of contradiction, the required predicate, and in so doing can at the same time become conscious of the necessity of the judgment—and that is what experience could never have taught me. On the other hand, though I do not include in the concept of a body in general the predicate 'weight', none the less this concept indicates an object of experience through one of its parts, and I can add to that part other parts of this same experience, as in this way belonging together with the concept. From the start I can apprehend the concept of body analytically through the characters of extension, impenetrability, figure, etc., all of which are thought in the concept. Now, however, looking back on the experience from which I have derived this concept of body, and finding weight to be invariably connected with the above characters, I attach it as a predicate to the concept; and in doing so I attach it synthetically, and am therefore extending my knowledge. The possibility of the synthesis of the predicate 'weight' with the concept of 'body' thus rests upon experience. While the one concept is not contained in the other, they yet belong to one another, though only contingently, as parts of a whole, namely, of an experience which is itself a synthetic combination of intuitions.

But in a priori synthetic judgments this help is entirely lacking. [I do not here have the advantage of looking around in the field of experience.] Upon what, then, am I to rely, when I seek to go beyond the concept A, and to know that another concept B is connected with it? Through what is the synthesis made possible? Let us take the proposition, 'Everything which happens has its cause'. In the concept of 'something which happens', I do indeed think an existence which is preceded by a time, etc., and from this concept analytic judgments may be obtained. But the concept of a 'cause' lies entirely outside the other concept, and signifies something different from 'that which happens', and is not therefore in any way contained in this latter representation. How come I then to predicate of that which happens something quite different, and to apprehend that the concept of cause, though not contained in it, yet belongs, and indeed necessarily belongs, to it? What is here the unknown $= X$ which gives support to the understanding when it believes that it can discover outside the concept A a predicate B foreign to this concept, which it yet at the same time considers to be connected with it? It cannot be experience, because the suggested principle has connected the second representation with the first, not only with greater universality, but also with the character of necessity, and therefore completely a priori and on the basis of mere concepts. Upon such synthetic, that is, ampliative principles, all our *a priori* speculative knowledge must ultimately rest; analytic judgments are very important, and indeed necessary, but only for obtaining that clearness in the concepts which is requisite for such a sure and wide synthesis as will lead to a genuinely new addition to all previous knowledge.

V. In All Theoretical Sciences of Reason Synthetic *A Priori* Judgments Are Contained as Principles

1. *All mathematical judgments, without exception, are synthetic.* This fact, though incontestably certain and in its consequences very important, has hitherto escaped the notice of those who are engaged in the analysis of human reason, and is, indeed, directly opposed to all their conjectures. For as it was found that all mathematical inferences proceed in accordance with the principle of contradiction (which the nature of all apodeictic certainty requires), it was supposed that the fundamental propositions of the science can themselves be known to be true through that principle. This is an erroneous view. For though a synthetic proposition can indeed be discerned in accordance with the principle of contradiction, this can only be if another synthetic proposition is presupposed, and if it can then be apprehended as following from this other proposition; it can never be so discerned in and by itself.

First of all, it has to be noted that mathematical propositions, strictly so called, are always judgments *a priori,* not empirical; because they carry with them necessity, which cannot be derived from experience. If this be demurred to, I am willing to limit my statement to *pure* mathematics, the very concept of which implies that it does not contain empirical, but only pure *a priori* knowledge.

We might, indeed, at first suppose that the proposition $7 + 5 = 12$ is a merely analytic proposition, and follows by the principle of contradiction from the concept of a sum of 7 and 5. But if we look more closely we find that the concept of the sum of 7 and 5 contains nothing save the union of the two numbers into one, and in this no thought is being taken as to what that single number may be which combines both. The concept of 12 is by no means already thought in merely thinking this union of 7 and 5; and I may analyse my concept of such a possible sum as long as I please, still I shall never find the 12 in it. We have to go outside these concepts, and call in the aid of the intuition which corresponds to one of them, our five fingers, for instance, or, as Segner does in his *Arithmetic,* five points, adding to the concept of 7, unit by unit, the five given in intuition. For starting with the number 7, and for the concept of 5 calling in the aid of the fingers of my hand as intuition, I now add one by one to the number 7 the units which I previously took together to form the number 5, and with the aid of that figure [the hand] see the number 12 come into being. That 5 should be added to 7, I have indeed already thought in the concept of a sum $= 7 + 5$, but not that this sum is equivalent to the number 12. Arithmetical propositions are therefore always synthetic. This is still more evident if we take larger numbers. For it is then obvious that, however we might turn and twist our concepts, we could never, by the mere analysis of them, and without the aid of intuition, discover what [the number is that] is the sum.

Just as little is any fundamental proposition of pure geometry analytic. That the straight line between two points is the shortest, is a synthetic proposition. For my concept of *straight* contains nothing of quantity, but only of quality. The concept of the shortest is wholly an addition, and cannot be derived, through any process of analysis, from the concept of the straight line. Intuition, therefore, must here be called in; only by its aid is the synthesis possible. What here causes us commonly to believe that the predicate of such apodeictic judgments is already contained in our concept, and that the judgment is therefore analytic, is merely the ambiguous character of the terms used. We are required to join in thought a certain predicate to a given concept, and this necessity is inherent in the concepts themselves. But the question is not what we *ought* to join in thought to the given concept, but what we *actually* think in it, even if only obscurely; and it is then manifest that, while the predicate is indeed attached necessarily to the concept, it is so in virtue of an intuition which must be added to the concept, not as thought in the concept itself.

Some few fundamental propositions, presupposed by the geometrician, are, indeed, really analytic, and rest on the principle of contradiction. But, as identical propositions, they serve only as links in the chain of method and not as principles; for instance, $a = a$; the whole is equal to itself; or $(a + b) > a$, that is, the whole is greater than its part. And even these propositions, though they are valid according to pure concepts, are only admitted in mathematics because they can be exhibited in intuition.

2. *Natural science* (*physics*) *contains* a priori *synthetic judgments as principles*. I need cite only two such judgments: that in all changes of the material world the quantity of matter remains unchanged; and that in all communication of motion, action and reaction must always be equal. Both propositions, it is evident, are not only necessary, and therefore in their origin *a priori*, but also synthetic. For in the concept of matter I do not think its permanence, but only its presence in the space which it occupies. I go outside and beyond the concept of matter, joining to it *a priori* in thought something which I have not thought *in* it. The proposition is not, therefore, analytic, but synthetic, and yet is thought *a priori;* and so likewise are the other propositions of the pure part of natural science.

3. *Metaphysics,* even if we look upon it as having hitherto failed in all its endeavours, is yet, owing to the nature of human reason, a quite indispensable science, and *ought to contain* a priori *synthetic knowledge*. For its business is not merely to analyse concepts which we make for ourselves *a priori* of things, and thereby to clarify them analytically, but to extend our *a priori* knowledge. And for this purpose we must employ principles which add to the given concept something that was not contained in it, and through *a priori* synthetic judgments venture out so far that experience is quite unable to follow us, as, for instance, in the proposition, that the world must have a first beginning, and such like. Thus metaphysics consists, at least *in intention,* entirely of *a priori* synthetic propositions.

Arthur Pap
(1921–1959)

Kant

*Pap presents a line-by-line exposition of Kant's distinction be-
tween analytic and synthetic truths and a priori and a posteriori
truths. He also treats some of the criticisms of Kant's handling
of these distinctions.*

A. A Priori Knowledge and Necessity

Kant's explicit definition of a priori knowledge is a negative
one: "knowledge that is independent of experience and even
of all sense impressions" (*Critique of Pure Reason,* 2d ed.,
intro., I).[1] The kind of independence in question is not, of
course, genetic, for Kant explicitly says that "undoubtedly all
our knowledge begins with experience." What he had in mind
is that a judgment is a priori if the *evidence* on which it is
accepted is not empirical. This leaves us, of course, with
"empirical" as an undefined term, but we must not deny to
an epistemologist the privilege of taking some terms as undefined in order to be able to define others (the meaning of
"empirical evidence" is, indeed, easily *illustrated,* by explaining, for example, that if the judgment "the straight line is the
shortest distance between two points" were empirical, then it
would be accepted on the evidence of repeated physical meas-
urements of length). Kant proceeds to formulate a *criterion* in
terms of which we can "infallibly distinguish pure (= a priori)
knowledge from empirical knowledge":

From Arthur Pap, *Semantics and Necessary Truth,* Chapter 2, pp. 22–42.
New Haven: Yale University Press, Inc., 1958. Copyright © 1958 by Yale
University Press, Inc. Reprinted by permission of the publisher.

[1] All translations from the German in this chapter are mine.

*If we find, in the first place, a proposition which is conceived
as necessary, then it is a judgment a priori; if, furthermore, it
is not derived from any other proposition which is itself necessarily valid, then it is absolutely a priori. Secondly, experience
never bestows on its judgments true or strict, but only supposed or comparative universality (through induction), so that
we should properly say: as far as our observations go, there
are no exceptions to this or that rule. If a judgment, then, is
thought as strictly universal, i.e. in such a way that no exception at all is admitted even as a possibility, then it is not derived from experience, but is absolutely a priori [intro., II].*

Little analysis is needed to see that Kant's two criteria really
coalesce into one, the criterion of necessity. For what does the
contrast between "strict" and "only supposed" universality
amount to? Kant surely does not mean that there are no universal empirical propositions that are true, i.e. that have no
exceptions. All he means is that we never know with certainty
that such a proposition is true, that there always remains the
possibility of its being false. But then a "strictly" universal
proposition is one which has no *conceivable* exceptions, which
is another way of saying that it is necessary. We may confine
our attention, therefore, to necessity as the touchstone of a
priori knowledge.

If we call "subjective" a property of a proposition *p* which is
such that to ascribe it to *p* is to say something about cognitive
attitudes toward *p*, then there can be no doubt that necessity,
and therewith a priori truth, in Kant's sense is a subjective
property of propositions. To say that *p* is necessary is to say
that *p* cannot be *conceived* to be false or is deducible from
propositions that cannot be conceived to be false. Indeed,
Kant explicitly says that in predicating a modality (such as
necessity) of a judgment, one does not add anything to the
"content" of the judgment but specifies the way in which the
relation of the components of the judgment (subject and predicate, or antecedent and consequent) is conceived.[2] As we

[2] Kant's own formulation is somewhat obscure: "The modality of judgment
is a very special function of theirs, whose distinguishing characteristic is
that it adds nothing to the content of the judgment (for besides quantity,
quality, and relation nothing is left as part of the content of the judgment),
but concerns only the value of the copula in relation to thought" (*Critique
of Pure Reason*, Transcendental Doctrine of Elements, Analytic of Conceptions, chap. 1, sec. 2). Especially is it not clear what he means by "content":
"*p* is possible" and "*p* is necessary," which are forms of positive modal
judgment, surely are not equivalent, and in that sense do not have the same
content. I think, however, his intention was to say that a modal judgment
Is about cognitive attitudes.

shall see, the attempts at explication of the concept of necessary truth which followed the Kantian era are characterized
precisely by the ambition to de-psychologize, if I may coin a
word, this concept, and one might say that to this extent their
Leitmotif was "back to Leibniz!" It must be said, however, in
all deference to the genius of Kant, that while *"p* cannot be
conceived to be false, or is deducible from propositions which
cannot be conceived to be false" seems to be the primary
meaning he attached to *"p* is necessary," it is impossible to
make Kant out as *consistent* in his usage of this central term.
When he says that it is a necessary (or a priori) truth that two
straight lines cannot enclose a space, or that the straight line
is the shortest distance between two points, he is clearly re-
ferring to the impossibility of imagining an exception. However, a serious deviation from the specified meaning can be
spotted in Kant's discussion of causality. In the very introduction to the *Critique of Pure Reason* where the difference between empirical and a priori knowledge is explained, Kant
cites the principle of causality, that every change has a cause,
as an example of a necessary proposition. In support of his
claim, made in criticism of Hume, that this is a *necessary* proposition he says: "indeed, in the latter (the proposition "every
change has a cause") the very concept of cause contains so
evidently the concept of a necessary connection with an effect
and of strict universality of the rule, that it would become entirely unrecognizable if one wanted, following Hume, to derive
it from a frequent conjunction of an event with a preceding
event and the resulting habit (and thus merely subjective
necessity) of association of ideas." What Kant maintains here
is that the concept of necessary connection is indispensable
for an adequate formulation of the principle of causality, thus:
"for every change there is an antecedent event which is necessarily connected with it." (The serious ambiguity, insufficiently
attended to by both Kant and Hume, that this might mean "for
every event there is an antecedent which is necessarily followed by the event" or "for every event there is an antecedent
which necessarily precedes the event" need not detain us in
this context.) But the principle, thus formulated, does not
entail that *it is necessary* that for every change there is an
antecedent event which is necessarily connected with it; in
other words, it is perfectly compatible with the proposition,
maintained by Hume, that it is conceivable that there should
occur a change which is uncaused in the sense that there is
no antecedent necessarily connected with it. It is, indeed,
unlikely that Kant intended to maintain the intuitive inconceiv-

ability of an uncaused change in the sense in which he maintained the intuitive inconceivability of a space that did not conform to the propositions of Euclidean geometry. As a matter of fact, the neo-Kantian interpreters of Kant have emphasized that Kant held the "principles of experience," of which the principle of causality is one, to be necessary in the sense of being *necessary presuppositions* of empirical science. This, however, is a complete shift of meaning of the term "necessary": from the fact that acceptance of proposition *p* is a *sine qua non* for the pursuit of inductive science, in the sense that from his very use of scientific method one can infer that the scientist believes *p*, it does not follow that *p* is a necessary proposition in the sense that it cannot be conceived to be false.

The poverty of the cited argument for the necessity of the principle of causality is clearly revealed if we consider that the same argument, if consistently employed, would have forced Kant into contradiction with his explicit admission that *specific causal laws,* unlike the principle of causality, are contingent propositions. For in line with his rejection of Hume's contention that the alleged necessary connection between cause and effect consists only in a "subjective necessity" (the pressure of the "gentle forces of association") he held that the concept of "objective necessity" is involved in a specific causal law like "the heat of solar radiation causes a block of ice to melt" just as it is involved in the general principle of causality. But then this specific causal law would have to be held to be a necessary proposition if the fact that the concept of necessary connection is a constituent of proposition *p* were a sufficient reason for holding *p* to be necessary. But quite apart from this consideration, the mentioned shift of meaning of the word "necessary" can be clearly traced in Kant's famous "proof" of the principle of causality in the section entitled "second analogy (of experience)." Kant observes that without the concept of causal order it would be impossible to distinguish objective and subjective temporal order of events. Mere perception, he says, is unable to determine the *objective order* of successive phenomena. For example, I might at this moment hear a voice and the next moment see the person whose lingual movements caused the sound; the effect, the sound, is perceived first, and the cause, the lingual movements, second. If I understand Kant (which is not easy), he is saying that in judging the lingual movements as the objectively earlier event I implicitly make the causal judgment that the lingual movements are the cause and the sound the effect. At any rate, Kant does maintain that if there were no causal order among a series of events $e_1, e_2 \ldots e_n$, then their *real* temporal relations would be indeterminate, it would be arbitrary whether we say e_1 is earlier than e_2 or e_2 earlier than e_1 or e_1 simultaneous with e_2. How he could maintain this in view of the (I should think) undeniable fact that we often agree that one event *really* preceded another event yet is causally unrelated to the latter, and that the proposition agreed upon is surely not self-contradictory (if it were, temporal sequence would be indistinguishable from causal sequence), I leave to the profounder Kant scholars to decide. For the sake of the argument, let us concede that the proposition that there is an objective temporal order of events entails the principle of causality. It is clear that this would amount only to a proof of the necessity of the proposition "if there is a real (objective) temporal order, then every event has a cause," but not to a proof of the necessity of the consequent of this conditional. In other words, what Kant would have proved at best is that the principle of causality is *necessarily presupposed* by the belief in an objective temporal order. He would not have established that a world devoid of objective temporal order— i.e., a world in which sometimes the impact of the stone is followed by the breaking of the window and sometimes follows the breaking of the window, in which a state of nonuniform density of a gas is sometimes followed by a state of uniform density and sometimes the reverse sequence occurs—is *intuitively inconceivable*. He is thus guilty of equivocation upon the term "necessity."

The central point to be kept in mind is that Kant's explicit distinction between the concepts of necessary and analytic truth made it impossible for him to adopt Leibniz' apparently nonpsychological criterion of necessary truth, the self-contradictoriness of the negation (in other words, the *logical* impossibility of exceptions). The alternative criterion which accommodates analytic truths as a subclass of necessary truths inevitably employs the wider concept of *inconceivability* (whether or not it be called "psychological"), for the word "possible" in Kant's statement "no exceptions (to an a priori truth) are admitted as possible" cannot mean what it meant for Leibniz: "consistent with the law of identity (or the law of contradiction)." However, if it were not for the tacit shift from "cannot be conceived to be false" to "necessarily presupposed by what is claimed as knowledge of objective reality," the extension of the term "necessary truth" would have been far smaller for

Kant than he claimed it to be, and much of his verbal disagreement with Hume would never have arisen.

B. The Definition of "Analytic"

It has often been pointed out that Kant's definition of an analytic judgment as a judgment whose predicate is (implicitly) contained in the concept of the subject (see *Critique of Pure Reason,* intro., IV) is unsatisfactory, not only because the literal meaning of the metaphor "contained" is not clear, but also because ever so many judgments (or propositions, as we say nowadays) do not have subject-predicate form and yet the analytic-synthetic division was intended by Kant as exhaustive with respect to the class of true propositions.[3] Let us first give our attention to the latter limitation. That Kant should not have been aware of it is particularly surprising since the table of the twelve different forms of judgments ("logical functions of the understanding") played such an important role in his doctrine of the categories. Take, for example, negative judgments, like "no triangle has four sides." Kant surely would have classified it as analytic, yet the predicate is so far from being contained in the subject that it contradicts the subject; the cited definition of "analytic," therefore, is restricted not only to judgments of subject-predicate form but even to affirmative judgments of that sort.[4] Again, existential judgments, like "there are cows," would no doubt have been classified as synthetic by Kant, yet the only way they could be construed as having subject-predicate form would be by treating existence as a predicate, which would be contrary to Kant's own famous thesis that existence is not a predicate. Again, consider hypothetical judgments, like "if somebody is somebody's teacher, then somebody is somebody's pupil" (which is reducible to a substitution-instance of a theorem of the logic of relations): Kant himself, in discussing the table of logical forms of judgments, mentions the relation of antecedent to consequent as distinct from the relation of subject to predicate; indeed, if the antece-

---

[3] *Self-contradictory* propositions, of course, are neither analytic nor synthetic in the Kantian senses of these terms; for this reason I characterize the divided class as the class of *true* propositions.

[4] Cf. on this point, Marc-Wogau's illuminating study "Kants Lehre vom Analytischen Urteil," *Theoria* 1951, Pts. I–III. Kant lifted, though, this particular restriction in the *Prolegomena,* § 2: "the predicate of an affirmative analytical judgment is already contained in the concept of the subject, . . . In the same way its opposite is necessarily denied of the subject in an analytical, but negative, judgment."

dent were construed as the "subject," then the expression "concept of the subject" would become unintelligible.

Fortunately, Kant also gave a criterion of analyticity (though he did not set it forth as a *definition*) which is at least potentially free from the restriction to subject-predicate propositions and which also has the virtue of being, at least *prima facie,* nonpsychological. The principle of contradiction ("Satz vom Widerspruch"), he says, while expressing a necessary condition of truth in general, expresses a sufficient condition of analytic truth: "If the judgment is *analytic,* be it negative or affirmative, then the principle of contradiction must always be a sufficient ground for ascertaining its truth" (*Critique of Pure Reason,* "On the Supreme Principle of All Analytical Judgments"). I deliberately said "potentially free" because the restriction to the subject-predicate form is apparent even in Kant's formulation of this principle: "no object has a predicate which contradicts it" ("Kelnem Dinge kommit ein Prädikat zu, welches ihm widerspricht"). It is not obvious, for example, how the statement "all *a* are *b,* but some *a* are not-*b"* is a violation of this principle: where is "object," where "predicate"? One might try to render the principle applicable by taking the class *a* as subject and "being wholly included in *b"* and "being partially excluded from *b"* as contradictory predicates. But this would be a tour de force, since the notions of class inclusion and class exclusion correspond to what was traditionally called the "copula" of a subject-predicate judgment, and so could not be used to form "predicates" in the traditional sense. It would be better to admit that Kant did not succeed in formulating a perfectly general principle of contradiction, i.e., one that is applicable to any form of proposition, but that if such a general version of the principle is substituted for Kant's, we have at least a criterion of analyticity that is not worse than Leibniz'. This general formulation is simply: $(p) - (p. - p)$, i.e. no proposition is both true and false.[5] Kant's intention, no doubt, was to say that an analytic proposition is a proposition from whose negation a contradiction, i.e. a statement of the form *"p* and not-*p"* is deducible.

In our discussion of Leibniz we have already pointed out that this is not satisfactory as a criterion of necessary truth, since "deducible" is presumably meant as short for "deducible with the help of necessary truths alone." But even as a

---

[5] This interpretation of the formula assumes the synonymy of *"- p"* and *"p* is false."

criterion of analytic truth in Kant's sense it faces a similar danger of circularity, which will become evident if we remember that the analytic-synthetic division was intended to exhaust the class of true propositions. For by implication, if not by explicit statement, Kant held the propositions of formal logic themselves to be analytic. Now, the principle of contradiction, as we have already seen, is by no means sufficient to demonstrate all propositions which both Leibniz and Kant would have classified as analytic. In order to obtain, therefore, a sufficiently wide criterion of analyticity, the reference to the principle of contradiction ought to give way to reference to the whole class of *logical truths: p* is analytic if a contradiction is derivable from not-*p* with the help of logical truths alone. Consider, for example, the conditional statement corresponding to the *tollendo tollens* form of argument: if *p* entails *q,* and not-*q,* then not-*p.* It is not immediately obvious that the negation of this complex statement violates the principle of contradiction in its generalized form. Close analysis reveals that in order to deduce an explicit contradiction (*p* and not-*p*) from it we require the law of double negation and, in order to show that *"p* and not-*q"* contradicts "it is impossible that *p* and not-*q"* (the negative version of *"p* entails *q"*), the axiom "if *p,* then *p* is possible." But now it turns out that it is not significant to characterize the truths of logic as being themselves analytic, since this would mean that from the negation of a logical truth one can deduce, with the help of logical truths, a contradiction—which is trivial, since we may simply use the negated logical truth along with its negation as a premise. And if, following the line of some modern philosophers, we say that the principles of logic are a priori *because* they are analytic, then we are talking nonsense if we use "analytic" in the specified sense.

In view of the difficulty . . . of defining a concept of analyticity which is at once distinct from the concept of a priori (or necessary) truth and allows us to say significantly that the principles of logic are analytic, the best course may be to restrict the range of significant application of the term "analytic" (and therewith of "synthetic") to statements which do not themselves belong to logic because they contain descriptive terms, like Kant's example "all bodies are extended." If so, then we have in the proposed reformulation of Kant's criterion of analytic truth a criterion which at least is not obscurer than the concept of logical truth itself.

Let us now turn our attention to the question of what exactly is the relation between subject and predicate in an analytic judgment according to Kant. In the *Prolegomena to Any Future Metaphysic* Kant improved on the cited definition from the *Critique* insofar as he dropped the metaphor "contained": "Analytical judgments express nothing in the predicate but what has been already actually thought in the concept of the subject, though not so distinctly or with the same (full) consciousness." The psychological language here used has been the focus of much criticism. For example, it has been said that the connotations of a term vary from individual to individual, and that therefore Kant's concept of analyticity is psychological. (It makes sense to say that "S is P" is analytic for so and so, but not to say simply " 'S is P' is analytic.") Consider, for example, Kant's claim that "all bodies are extended" is analytic while "all bodies have weight" is synthetic; just how would Kant prove, so the objection runs, that people are not thinking of weight when they think of a body? Kant would, of course, admit that, by virtue of what Hume called "habits of association," the thought of a body is *accompanied* by the thought of weight, just as the thought of a dog might be accompanied by the thought of barking. But he would deny that having weight is part of the *meaning* of "body." And he would, had he been reared in the language of contemporary analytic philosophers, support this claim by appeal to the fact that the concept of a weightless body (unlike that of a body devoid of inertia) is *not self-contradictory;* or that "x is a body" does not analytically *entail* (though it may factually imply, i.e. imply by virtue of an empirical law) "x has weight." If Kant's conception of analyticity, then, is to be condemned as "psychologistic," at least he will enjoy the company of many subtle contemporary analysts of reputation. When we argue nowadays "it does not seem self-contradictory to suppose that a body existed all alone in space, and since weight is a relation of a body to other bodies (consisting in its being attracted to other bodies), it follows that weight is not part of what is *meant* by 'body,' " we equally rely on "thought experiments."

The problem of philosophical semantics which is implicit in Kant's statement about the relation of subject and predicate in analytic judgments is simply the problem of what a suitable criterion of *identity* (total or partial) *of concepts* might be. That Kant failed to solve this problem is surely a forgivable sin if one considers that the entire problem of the identity conditions of intensions (when are two properties identical, when are two propositions identical?) is still highly controversial nowadays in spite of the professed rejection of "psychologism" in philosophical semantics. In his study referred to above, Marc-Wogau concentrates on just this difficulty with Kant's doctrine of the analytic judgment. Consider the judgment "every triangle has three angles." It would not help to say that "having three angles" is a constituent of the concept "triangle" if and only if it occurs in the *definition* of "triangle," for thus the burden would merely be placed on the question "what is meant by *the* definition of a concept?" We might define "triangle" to mean "plane figure bounded by three straight lines and having three angles"; in that case the judgment would be analytic by the above criterion of partial identity of subject and predicate. But it would commonly be said that such a definition involves a redundancy: "plane figure bounded by three straight lines" is sufficient, one would say, since the other property is *deducible* from this definition. But in what sense is it "deducible?" The situation is not quite analogous to the redundancy in the definiens for "square": equilateral, four-sided rectangle; for here the redundant predicate "four-sided" can be extracted simply by defining "rectangle" ("four-sided rectilinear figure all of whose angles are right angles"), while "triangular" is not in the same straightforward sense contained in the definiens of "trilateral." Perhaps a formal deduction of *"x is triangular"* from *"x is trilateral"* requires the theorem "if a closed figure has *n* sides, then it has *n* angles," but if *"P is contained in S"* is used in the sense of *"P* is deducible from the definition of *S* together with axioms or theorems of the system in which *S* is defined," then we obtain of course a concept of analyticity which is far wider than the one Kant had in mind ("all triangles have as the sum of their angles 180 degrees" could be analytic in that sense!) and which, moreover, turns "analytic" into a term relative to a deductive system, which was definitely not Kant's intention. Kant, then, would be hard pressed were he asked whether the concept "triangle" is adequately defined as "rectilinear figure with three sides and three angles" or as "rectilinear figure with three sides" or as "rectilinear figure with three angles."[6]

Since the interpretation of *"P* is contained in *S"* as meaning *"P* occurs either directly or indirectly—through expansion of definienda into definientia—in the definiens of *the definition* of *S"* comes nearest to giving an objective meaning to Kant's

---

[6] Amusingly, as Marc-Wogau brings out, Kant was inconsistent in his claims as to what is to be regarded as the definition of "triangle." See *loc. cit.*, p. 151.

term "analytic," it is with considerable curiosity that we look to Kant's own statements about the nature of definitions.

In the *Critique* we read, in the section entitled "The discipline of Pure Reason in its Dogmatic Use" (Transcendental Doctrine of Method, chap. I, sect. I): "As the very term 'to define' indicates, to define means nothing more than to express the complete concept of an object within its limits and in underived manner." The explanations of the terms "complete" and "within limits," given in a footnote, make it clear that Kant meant to say that the definiens must express, in clear language, a necessary and sufficient condition for applicability of the concept, and must contain no redundancy; and by the requirement of "Ursprünglichkeit" is meant, as he explains in the same footnote, that the defining property should not stand in need of demonstration. It is obvious that Kant had the Aristotelian distinction between essence and property in mind, according to which "a plane figure with the sum of its angles equal to 180 degrees" could not serve as definiens for "triangle" because, even though it is convertibly predicable of triangles, it does not express the *essence* of triangularity but rather "flows" from the latter. And since to clarify Kant's concept of analyticity is the same as to clarify the expression "essence of a concept," this explanation get us nowhere; in fact, the notion of essence is made no clearer by Kant than it was by Aristotle himself. In his *Logic* (*Vorlesungen zur Logik*) he makes the traditional distinction between *nominal* and *real* definitions (§ 106). But it is simply impossible to make any consistent sense of his disconnected remarks on the distinction.[7] A nominal definition, we are told, is an arbitrary stipulation of a meaning for a given name, while a real definition demonstrates the possibility of the defined object from its "inner" marks (I have nowhere found as much as a hint of the meaning of "inner"). Real definitions, we are told, are to be found in mathematics, "for the definition of an arbitrary concept is always real." What Kant elsewhere says about mathematical concepts leaves no doubt that "arbitrary concept" here means "constructed concept." The mathematician, Kant held (following Locke, whose distinction between ideas of substances and ideas of modes must have influenced him more than he liked to admit),[8] does not abstract his concepts from

---

[7] And since Kant authorized the publication of these lecture notes, we cannot hold his students responsible for this blemish.

[8] Cf. the self-conscious confession of indebtedness to Locke in the *Prolegomena,* § 3.

empirical objects but *constructs* them prior to experience of instances. But consider, then, the definition of "ellipsoid" as meaning "solid generated by rotating an ellipse around either one of its axes," where "ellipse" is similarly given a genetic definition, viz. "closed curve all of whose points are such that the sum of their distances from two fixed points is constant" (this definition is usually called analytic but Kant would have called it "genetic" because we can derive from it a recipe as to how an ellipse might be constructed). This is undoubtedly the sort of thing Kant had in mind when speaking of the real definitions of constructed mathematical concepts which guarantee the possibility of the defined object since we can, following the recipe, construct on the blackboard or on white paper objects satisfying them. Yet if the definiendum "ellipsoid" has no antecedent usage and has just been invented as an abbreviation for the complex definiens, then the same definition is nominal according to the explanation given! The carelessness of Kant's thinking (or at least lecturing) on the nature of definitions is sufficiently illustrated by this point, and we must therefore conclude that to the extent to which the meaning of Kant's "analytic" depends on the meaning of *"the* definition of the subject-concept," it is obscure.

Before leaving the subject, I would like to call attention to a most interesting observation made by Marc-Wogau, connected with Kant's statement that, strictly speaking, concepts of natural kinds, like gold, cannot be defined at all:

For, as an empirical concept consists only of a few marks of a certain kind of object of the senses, it is never certain whether one might not mean by a word denoting an identical object at one time more, at another time fewer marks of the object. Thus one person's concept of gold might contain, besides the weight, the color and the solidity, the property of being uncapable of rusting, while another person may not know this property. A fixed set of marks is used only as long as they suffice for the purpose of distinguishing the kind from others; through new discoveries, however, some marks get removed and some get added, and consequently the concept is never perfectly fixed [Critique of Pure Reason, loc. cit.].

Marc-Wogau comments that thus the sentence "gold does not get rusty in water" is analytic for the first person, synthetic for the second. Similarly, an identity sentence of the form "$a=$ the x with property P" (where "a" is a proper name) might be said to be analytic for a person in whose usage "a" is precisely an abbreviation for that description, and synthetic for a person using the same proper name as abbreviation for another description which, though denoting the same object as the first, is based on a predicate Q which is not synonymous with P. However, is all that Kant's apperçu amounts to that the same class term may be given different definitions by different people, such that instead of saying "S is analytic" we ought to say "S is analytic *as used* by X"? It rather seems that Kant saw, though none too clearly, that statements about natural kinds, like "gold is yellow," cannot be classified as analytic or synthetic in the sense in which statements about mathematical objects are so classifiable, for the reason that "analytic" was defined in terms of "definition," and there can be no "definitions" of natural kinds in the same sense of the word as there can be definitions of mathematical concepts. To be sure, Kant did not clearly explain *why* concepts of natural kinds should not be "strictly definable." But perhaps he could have made his point as follows. Suppose that "gold" were defined as a yellow metal with a definite atomic weight and a definite melting point. If this were a "definition" in the same sense in which " 'square' means 'equilateral rectangle' " is a definition, then it would be self-contradictory to classify an object which had all the defining characteristics except the color as gold, just as it would be self-contradictory to classify, say, a rhombus as a square. If a scientist observing such an anomalous specimen insisted, "Still, this *is* gold, so we must recognize that not all gold is yellow," he would have to be interpreted as recommending a redefinition of "gold," not as pronouncing an empirical generalization refuted. But if he said instead, "This is not a species of gold, it's a different species though closely similar to gold," this, would likewise be an acceptable comment. Just which way the discovery of the goldlike, hitherto unknown, specimen will affect his classification of natural kinds will depend on pragmatic considerations. Now, Kant might hold that no analogous situation could occur in connection with geometrical and arithmetical concepts, that there could be no occasion for "redefining" such concepts in the light of new discoveries about their instances; and that this suggests that "definition" does not have the same meaning in "definition of 'gold' " as in "definition of 'square.' "

**C. Synthetic A Priori Truth
in Geometry**

Of all the synthetic a priori propositions alleged as such by Kant, those that illustrate his conception of an a priori truth as a universal proposition exceptions to which are *inconceivable* most clearly are geometrical axioms, like the famous axiom "two straight lines cannot enclose a space." In fact, if one were pressed to explain the relevant meaning of the word "inconceivable," one might well do it denotatively by giving such examples as the inconceivability of a space enclosed by two straight lines. As to the *intuitive* nature of geometrical knowledge Kant made two claims: first, that our knowledge of the axioms is intuitive ("intuitive" being contrasted with both "empirical" and "analytic"), and secondly, that even the deduction of theorems from the axioms requires spatial intuition. The latter claim was not any more far-fetched than the former, considering the role played by *constructions* in the proofs of Euclidean geometry such as the proof of the theorem about the sum of the angles of a triangle (see particularly the *Critique,* "Transcendental Doctrine of Method," chap. 1, sec. 1). However, Kant here failed to make the distinction, often urged nowadays, between the context of *discovery* and the context of *justification.* If it were granted that constructions are indispensable for the discovery of proofs, it still would not follow that recourse to constructions is required for validating a proof once discovered. Hilbert has shown that if only all the axioms tacitly assumed by Euclid in his proofs are made fully explicit, then purely *formal* proofs of the theorems can be given. We shall concentrate, accordingly, on the former claim, of the inconceivability of the falsehood of the Euclidean axioms. It has been exposed to heavy fire since the publication of non-Euclidean systems of geometry discredited Kant's doctrine of the finality of Euclidean geometry. We shall begin with the question of whether the axioms are a priori, and then turn to the question whether they are synthetic.

A rather naive argument against the claim of self-evidence for an axiom like "two straight lines cannot enclose a space," which is nevertheless often advanced, is that this proposition has even been shown to be false, since it does not hold in Riemannian geometry; which geometry is actually suited for the description of physical space if only we consider sufficiently large areas. Now, it is clear that if a system of pure geometry contains the contradictory of the sentence "a straight line is uniquely determined by two points," the term "straight line" does not in that system mean what it means in the system containing the contradicted sentence. For to the extent that the primitives "point," "straight line," "plane" have any meanings at all as part of such an uninterpreted system of geometry, they mean whatever entities satisfy the axioms, and the same entities cannot satisfy mutually contradictory axiom sets. For example, Reimannian "straight lines" can be interpreted as great arcs on a spherical surface, and with this interpretation it becomes true to say that two straight lines may enclose a space. But it is not then the *proposition* expressed by the sentence "two straight lines cannot enclose a space" in the Euclidean system which has been contradicted. Those who are anxious to defend the thesis that all a priori truth is analytic may seize the opportunity to point out that what on this analysis is an a priori truth is the proposition that two *Euclidean* straight lines cannot enclose a space, which is analytic because "Euclidean" can be defined only in terms of satisfaction of just such axioms as the one in question. But discussion of the tricky question whether the axiom is analytic or synthetic had better be postponed until careful attention has been given to the question of whether any of the arguments against the *necessity* of the axiom are sound.

A well known objection—one, indeed, which people are apt to echo in rather thoughtless manner just because it is "classic"—is that inconceivability is altogether relative to experience and accepted scientific theory. It is said again and again that the history of science amply proves that what is self-evident to one generation is rejected as false by the next generation on the authority of well-confirmed scientific theory. And the classical example of this is the question of the conceivability of antipodes. Thus John Stuart Mill, in the context of arguing for the empirical character of geometrical truths, writes:

There are remarkable instances of this in the history of science; instances in which the most instructed men rejected as impossible, because inconceivable, things which their posterity, by earlier practice and longer perseverance in the attempt, found it quite easy to conceive, and which everybody now knows to be true. There was a time when men of the most cultivated intellects, and the most emancipated from the dominion of early prejudice, could not credit the existence of antipodes; were unable to conceive, in opposition to old association, the force of gravity acting upward instead of downward [System of Logic (*1887*), *Bk. II, chap. 5, § 6*].

But this argument, plausible as it sounds, is spoiled by an ambiguity of the word "conceivable." That people on diametrically opposite points of a sphere should both remain attached to that sphere without any tendency to "fall off" is inconceivable in the same sense in which it is inconceivable that a person could walk on the surface of a lake, or that a person could jump off a cliff and find himself rising instead of falling. Here "inconceivable" means "unbelievable" but not "unimaginable." Experience has developed in us an irresistible tendency to expect *A* to be followed by *B,* but if we did not admit that an exception is in some sense imaginable, it would be difficult to explain what we mean by saying that *"A is always followed by B"* is a *contingent* (or *empirical*) truth. That people ever found the existence of antipodes unimaginable in the sense in which a space enclosed by two Euclidean straight lines, or a space of four dimensions (in the ordinary, not the generalized, sense of "space"), is unimaginable, is a wildly unplausible assumption; at any rate, the historical evidence that they declared this sort of thing "impossible" or "inconceivable" is not relevant, since we declare many things impossible or inconceivable which we find it impossible to *believe* but which we can *imagine,* or *think of,* without excessive difficulty. Who could believe that there is a man who will never die? But who has serious difficulty in forming the concept of an immortal man, or even of a man whose appearance remains unaltered during a thousand years?[9]

Curiously, Mill admits that once we have acquired through experience with straight lines the notion of straightness, mere reflection upon this notion suffices for revealing the truth of the axiom. He approvingly quotes Bain's statement (as going "to the very root of the controversy"): "We cannot have the full meaning of Straightness, without going through a comparison of straight objects among themselves, and with their opposites, bent or crooked objects. The result of this comparison is, *inter alia,* that straightness in two lines is seen to

---

[9] Unfortunately Whewell, whose doctrine of the necessity of geometrical axioms Mill attacked, was himself guilty of this equivocation on the term "inconceivable" (as meaning sometimes "unimaginable" and sometimes "unbelievable"), and for this reason Mill's criticism is much more persuasive than it would otherwise be. Thus Mill cites with considerable glee Whewell himself as reporting that such revolutionary theories as the Copernican, and Galileo's theory of uniform motion as not requiring to be sustained by force, were at the time rejected as inconceivable.

be incompatible with inclosing a space; the inclosure of space involves crookedness in at least one of the lines" (*System of Logic*, § 5). But if the fact that reflection on the meaning of a sentence *S* is sufficient to produce assent to *S* does not prove that *S* expresses an a priori truth, what could "a priori truth" mean? Mill may have been right in holding, following Locke and Hume, that such geometrical concepts as straightness are derived from sense impressions of straightness (and in that sense are empirical concepts), but it surely is possible for a necessary proposition to contain empirical concepts. It appears, then, that it is rather obscure what Mill was denying when he denied that the axiom in question is a *necessary* truth. And similarly we must challenge anyone who, while admitting that enclosure of a space by two straight lines cannot be imagined in the sense in which dogs that can fly and speak French can be imagined, denies that the axiom is a necessary truth, to explain what he means by a "necessary truth."

There are those who hold that if the negation of a proposition is inconceivable in an absolute sense, i.e. not just in the sense that habits of association produced by experience make it *psychologically* impossible to believe it, this can only be because the proposition is definitionally true, "analytic." Since "*p* is definitionally true" means presumably that *p* is deducible from logical principles (such as the principle of identity) with the help of adequate definitions, it would indeed be difficult to explain the absolute inconceivability of the negation of a logical principle in the same way. But be this as it may, let us see whether Kant can be successfully refuted by proving that such a geometrical axiom is analytic. We may formulate the axiom as an axiom of plane geometry as follows: two straight lines have either no point in common or else exactly one. When Kant pronounced it as "synthetic" he could hardly have had in mind his definition of a synthetic judgment as one whose predicate is not contained in the subject, for if there are any propositions which do not have subject-predicate form, this is one. Let us, then, take "analytic" in the sense Kant must have intended when he said that the principle of contradiction is the sufficient ground of analytic judgments: the judgment cannot be denied without self-contradiction. The difficulty faced by the claim that our axiom is analytic in this sense is that the only explicit definition of "straight line" which would enable a proof of analyticity is one which Kant would have regarded as itself a synthetic axiom: a straight line is a line which is uniquely determined by two points (i.e.

given two points, there is one and only one straight line containing both).[10] Given this definition, the axiom could indeed be formally demonstrated: if two straight lines did have two points in common, then there would be two distinct straight lines containing two given points, which contradicts the definition of "straight line." The fact that a definition which seems perfectly adequate could be rejected by a Kantian as question begging—since on the same general grounds on which he regards the axiom to be demonstrated as synthetic he would hold the definition to express a synthetic judgment—is indeed a forceful reminder that, unless one can clarify the relevant sense of "adequate definition," the concept of analyticity is hopelessly obscure. But let us see whether there is some way in which a Kantian could be forced to surrender. One might argue that since "straight line" has different meanings in different systems of geometry, we have to fix the relevant concept by specifying a definite kind of plane, thus: "straight line in a Euclidean plane," "straight line in a Riemannian plane," etc. We would then be led to the question of what is meant by "Euclidean plane." Now, a type of plane, so we might argue, can be defined in no other way than as the type of plane for which the axioms of a given plane geometry hold. More precisely, the idea is this: we formulate the axioms "two straight lines in P have either no point or exactly one point in common," "given a point in P and a straight line in P not containing that point, there is exactly one straight line in P which contains that point and has no point in common with the given straight line," and others. So far the axioms are propositional functions, neither true nor false, since they contain the variable "P"; hence it would not make sense to ask whether they are analytic or synthetic. But the only way "P" could be given a meaning that guarantees the truth of the axioms would be by the definition "P is whatever satisfies these axioms." Now the axiom will read "two straight lines in a plane in which two straight lines have either no point in common or exactly one point in common have either no point in common or exactly one point in common," which is surely analytic. But the trouble with this trick is that it leads us into a circle. For a type of plane has been defined in terms of "straight line," but our starting consideration was that "straight line" is ambiguous until a definite type of plane is specified.

---

[10] Kant mentions somewhere that the proposition "three points uniquely determine a plane" is synthetic, hence one would expect him to hold the same view with respect to the analogous proposition about the straight line.

It is difficulties of this sort that presumably led such mathematicians as Hilbert to abandon the quest for *explicit* definitions of the terms "straight line," "point," "plane," and instead to define them implicitly as whatever entities satisfy the formal axioms formulated by means of them. The Kant critique since Hilbert accordingly took the form that the axioms of *pure* geometry are neither analytic nor synthetic, for they are propositional functions, not propositions. The question arises of whether this may be regarded as a refutation of Kant, and this is to ask whether Kant meant by *pure* geometry what is nowadays meant by it. The question answers itself: Kant, after all, lived *before* Hilbert. But is it possible to make the meaning of "pure geometry" intended by *Kant* intelligible?

It seems clear that the Kantian concept of "pure geometry" can be defined only in terms of the notion, going back to Plato, of *a priori concepts* ("innate ideas"). An a priori concept would have to be defined as a concept which, though it is not purely formal (like the logical constants, "not," "implication," etc.), is neither ostensively definable nor analytically definable in terms of ostensively definable concepts. That Kant thought of "straight line" as just such an a priori concept cannot be doubted by anyone who is aware of the impression which Plato's theory of innate ideas (whatever its cognitive content may be) must have made on Kant via Descartes. Kant would say that no instance of a perfect straight line could be given in sense perception ("empirical intuition"); hence ostensive definition is out of the question. But I think that he moreover held the concept to be unanalyzable, a *simple* concept. For his proof of the synthetic character of the axiom "the straight line is the shortest distance between two points" is that the subject-concept is purely qualitative while the predicate is quantitative. Yet any conceivable analysis of "straight line" would have to be in what Kant would call "quantitative terms: "class of points which is uniquely determined by *two* points" is quantitative too! But by the same argument Kant should even have denied that the statement "the circle is a closed curve all of whose points are equidistant from a given point" is analytic: if we understand what Kant means by saying that straightness is a *quality,* we must surely confess that circularity is in the same sense a quality. Now, if Kant were asked why on earth he rejects such definitions as not really *analyzing* the subject-concept, he would, I think, make the reply that you could not teach someone the meaning of the terms "straight" and "circular" by means of such quantitative descriptions unless he had, stimulated by sense experience, already acquired these concepts. If so, then Kant implicitly used the expression "analysis of concept *C*" in such a way that a given definition could be said to express an analysis of *C* only if it is possible to make a person who had never experienced an instance of *C* think of *C* by producing that definition. Thus "color between yellow and blue" would not express an analysis of the concept *green* if it is impossible to make a person who has not seen green before think of green by means of that description.

Supposing that "straight line" and "point," as used in pure geometry in Kant's sense of "pure," express such simple a priori concepts (dispositions, perhaps, to remember intellectual visions enjoyed in Plato's heaven of Forms), what follows with regard to the question of whether the axioms of such a pure geometry are analytic or synthetic? If "*S* is analytic" means "*S* is deducible from logical truths *with the help of adequate analyses* of the terms of *S*," and the relevant terms of *S* are not analyzable at all, does it then follow that *S* is synthetic? It seems to me that the question does not admit of a nonarbitrary answer, because philosophers have not taken the trouble to specify whether the statement "*S* is *not* deducible from logical truths with the help of adequate analyses" is to be taken as true in case no adequate analyses of the relevant terms can be produced at all. It is somewhat like the question of whether a man who never beat his wife has or has not stopped beating her. In fact, as we have seen, Kant himself raised the question of what sorts of concepts are definable at all—though he sadly neglected to clarify the relevant meaning of "definable"—and maintained that concepts of natural kinds, for example, are not definable. This did not prevent him from declaring elsewhere that "gold is yellow" is an analytic judgment. In the same way, his implicit view that "straight line" is not definable did not prevent him from declaring that "the straight line is the shortest distance between two points" is *not* analytic. What he did not consider was the possibility that the division analytic-synthetic is not significantly applicable to statements whose relevant terms are unanalyzable.[11]

[11] Although a suitable restriction of the class of statements to which the analytic-synthetic dichotomy applies would spare philosophers some embarrassment, no such restrictions are usually considered by philosophers operating with the dichotomy. In particular, the supposed unanalyzability of the relevant predicates in a given statement is usually regarded as a basis for classifying the statement as synthetic. Thus ethical intuitionists who hold ethical predicates like "right" and "good" to be unanalyzable pronounce statements connecting such predicates with naturalistic predicates for this very reason as synthetic.

John Stuart Mill
(1806–1873)

Of Demonstration, and Necessary Truths

Kant was convinced that there has to be a category of truths **53**
which are not contingent like our example A (see Introduction)
in that they are not subject to disconfirmation by what goes
on in the world, but neither are they true in virtue of their form
(example B) or "by definition" (example C). Of special interest
is the question of whether mathematical truths (i.e., such
propositions as **7 + 5 = 12)** *are of this special category. Kant*
argued that they were; Hobbes did not see the need for a
third category, arguing that mathematical truths were true by
definition, like **no grandmother is childless.** *Mill also thought*
that there was no need for a third category, but he thought
that mathematical truths were like **all that glitters is not gold**
that is, in *fact* true *but subject to disconfirmation by what hap-*
pens in the world.

If, as laid down in the two preceding chapters, the foundation
of all sciences, even deductive or demonstrative sciences, is
Induction; if every step in the ratiocinations even of geometry
is an act of induction; and if a train of reasoning is but bringing many inductions tó bear upon the same subject of inquiry,
and drawing a case within one induction by means of another;
wherein lies the peculiar certainty always ascribed to the
sciences which are entirely, or almost entirely, deductive?
Why are they called the Exact Sciences? Why are mathematical certainty, and the evidence of demonstration, common
phrases to express the very highest degree of assurance at-
tainable by reason? Why are mathematics by almost all phi-

From John Stuart Mill, *A System of Logic,* Vol. I, Chapter V and VI of
Book II, pp. 258–262, 273–285, 290–297. London: Longmans, Green and Co.,
1879.

losophers, and (by some) even those branches of natural philosophy which, through the medium of mathematics, have been converted into deductive sciences, considered to be independent of the evidence of experience and observation, and characterized as systems of Necessary Truth?

The answer I conceive to be, that this character of necessity, ascribed to the truths of mathematics and even (with some reservations to be hereafter made) the peculiar certainty attributed to them, is an illusion; in order to sustain which, it is necessary to suppose that those truths relate to, and express the properties of purely imaginary objects. It is acknowledged that the conclusions of geometry are deduced, partly at least, from the so-called Definitions, and that those definitions are assumed to be correct representations, as far as they go, of the objects with which geometry is conversant. Now we have pointed out that, from a definition as such, no proposition, unless it be one concerning the meaning of a word, can ever follow; and that what apparently follows from a definition, follows in reality from an implied assumption, that there exists a real thing conformable thereto. This assumption in the case of the definitions of geometry, is not strictly true: there exist no real things exactly conformable to the definitions. There exist no points without magnitude; no lines without breadth, nor perfectly straight; no circles with all their radii exactly equal, nor squares with all their angles perfectly right. It will perhaps be said that the assumption does not extend to the actual, but only to the possible, existence of such things. I answer that, according to any test we have of possibility, they are not even possible. Their existence, so far as we can form any judgment, would seem to be inconsistent with the physical constitution of our planet at least, if not of the universal. To get rid of this difficulty, and at the same time to save the credit of the supposed system of necessary truth, it is customary to say that the points, lines, circles, and squares which are the subject of geometry, exist in our conceptions merely, and are part of our minds; which minds, by working on their own materials, construct an à priori science, the evidence of which is purely mental, and has nothing whatever to do with outward experience. By howsoever high authorities this doctrine may have been sanctioned, it appears to me psychologically incorrect. The points, lines, circles, and squares which any one has in his mind, are (I apprehend) simply copies of the points, lines, circles, and squares which he has known in his experience. Our idea of a point, I apprehend to be simply our idea of the *minimum visibile,* the smallest portion of surface which we can see. A line as defined by geometers is wholly inconceivable. We can reason about a line as if it had no breadth; because we have a power, which is the foundation of all the control we can exercise over the operations of our minds; the power, when a perception is present to our senses or a conception to our intellects, of *attending* to a part only of that perception or conception, instead of the whole. But we cannot *conceive* a line without breadth; we can form no mental picture of such a line: all the lines which we have in our minds are lines possessing breadth. If any one doubts this, we may refer him to his own experience. I much question if any one who fancies that he can conceive what is called a mathematical line, thinks so from the evidence of his consciousness: I suspect it is rather because he supposes that unless such a conception were possible, mathematics could not exist as a science: a supposition which there will be no difficulty in showing to be entirely groundless.

Since, then, neither in nature, nor in the human mind, do there exist any objects exactly corresponding to the definitions of geometry, while yet that science cannot be supposed to be conversant about non-entities; nothing remains but to consider geometry as conversant with such lines, angles, and figures, as really exist; and the definitions, as they are called, must be regarded as some of our first and most obvious generalizations concerning those natural objects. The correctness of those generalizations, *as* generalizations, is without a flaw: the equality of all the radii of a circle is true of all circles, so far as it is true of any one: but it is not exactly true of any circle; it is only nearly true; so nearly that no error of any importance in practice will be incurred by feigning it to be exactly true. When we have occasion to extend these inductions, or their consequences, to cases in which the error would be appreciable—to lines of perceptible breadth or thickness, parallels which deviate sensibly from equidistance, and the like—we correct our conclusions, by combining with them a fresh set of propositions relating to the aberration; just as we also take in propositions relating to the physical or chemical properties of the material, if those properties happen to introduce any modification into the result; which they easily may, even with respect to figure and magnitude, as in the case, for instance, of expansion by heat. So long, however, as there exists no practical necessity for attending to any of the properties of the object except its geometrical properties, or to any of the natural irregularities in those, it is convenient to neglect the consideration of the other properties and of the irregularities, and to reason as if these did not exist: accordingly, we formally announce in the definitions, that we intend to proceed on this plan. But it is an error to suppose, because we resolve to confine our attention to a certain number of the properties of an object, that we therefore conceive, or have an idea of, the object denuded of its other properties. We are thinking, all the time, of precisely such objects as we have seen and touched, and with all the properties which naturally belong to them; but for scientific convenience, we feign them to be divested of all properties, except those which are material to our purpose, and in regard to which we design to consider them.

The peculiar accuracy, supposed to be characteristic of the first principles of geometry, thus appears to be fictitious. The assertions on which the reasonings of the science are founded, do not, any more than in other sciences, exactly correspond with the fact; but we suppose that they do so, for the sake of tracing the consequences which follow from the supposition. The opinion of Dugald Stewart respecting the foundations of geometry, is, I conceive, substantially correct; that it is built on hypotheses; that it owes to this alone the peculiar certainty supposed to distinguish it; and that in any science whatever, by reasoning from a set of hypotheses, we may obtain a body of conclusions as certain as those of geometry, that is, as strictly in accordance with the hypotheses, and as irresistibly compelling assent, on condition that those hypotheses are true.[1]

When, therefore, it is affirmed that the conclusions of geometry are necessary truths, the necessity consists in reality

[1] It is justly remarked by Professor Bain (Logic, ii. 134) that the word Hypothesis is used here in a somewhat peculiar sense. An hypothesis, in science, usually means a supposition not proved to be true, but surmised to be so because if true it would account for certain known facts; and the final result of the speculation may be to prove its truth. The hypotheses spoken of in the text are of a different character; they are known not to be literally true, while as much of them as is true is not hypothetical, but certain. The true cases, however, resemble in the circumstance that in both we reason, not from a truth, but from an assumption, and the truth therefore of the conclusions is conditional, not categorical. This suffices to justify, in point of logical propriety, Stewart's use of the term. It is of course needful to bear in mind that the hypothetical element in the definitions of geometry is the assumption that what is very nearly true is exactly so. This unreal exactitude might be called a fiction, as properly as an hypothesis; but that appellation, still more than the other, would fail to point out the close relation which exists between the fictitious point or line and the points and lines of which we have experience.

only in this, that they correctly follow from the suppositions from which they are deduced. Those suppositions are so far from being necessary, that they are not even true; they purposely depart, more or less widely, from the truth. The only sense in which necessity can be ascribed to the conclusions of any scientific investigation, is that of legitimately following from some assumption, which, by the conditions of the inquiry, is not to be questioned. In this relation, of course, the derivative truths of every deductive science must stand to the inductions, or assumptions, on which the science is founded, and which, whether true or untrue, certain or doubtful in themselves, are always supposed certain for the purposes of the particular science. And therefore the conclusions of all deductive sciences were said by the ancients to be necessary propositions. We have observed already that to be predicated necessarily was characteristic of the predicable Proprium, and that a proprium was any property of a thing which could be deduced from its essence, that is, from the properties included in its definition. . . .

The first of the two arguments in support of the theory that axioms are a *priori* truths, having, I think, been sufficiently answered; I proceed to the second, which is usually the most relied on. Axioms (it is asserted) are conceived by us not only as true, but as universally and necessarily true. Now, experience cannot possibly give to any proposition this character. I may have seen snow a hundred times, and may have seen that it was white, but this cannot give me entire assurance even that all snow is white; much less that snow *must* be white. "However many instances we may have observed of the truth of a proposition, there is nothing to assure us that the next case shall not be an exception to the rule. If it be strictly true that every ruminant animal yet known has cloven hoofs, we still cannot be sure that some creature will not hereafter be discovered which has the first of these attributes, without having the other. . . . Experience must always consist of a limited number of observations; and, however numerous these may be, they can show nothing with regard to the infinite number of cases in which the experiment has not been made." Besides, Axioms are not only universal, they are also necessary. Now "experience cannot offer the smallest ground for the necessity of a proposition. She can observe and record what has happened; but she cannot find, in any case, or in any accumulation of cases, any reason for what *must* happen. She may see objects side by side; but she cannot see a reason why they must ever be side by side. She finds certain events to occur in succession; but the succession supplies, in its occurrence, no reason for its recurrence. She contemplates external objects; but she cannot detect any internal bond, which indissolubly connects the future with the past, the possible with the real. To learn a proposition by experience, and to see it to be necessarily true, are two altogether different processes of thought."[2] And Dr. Whewell adds, "If any one does not clearly comprehend this distinction of necessary and contingent truths, he will not be able to go along with us in our researches into the foundations of human knowledge; nor, indeed, to pursue with success any speculation on the subject."[3]

In the following passage, we are told what the distinction is, the non-recognition of which incurs this denunciation. "Necessary truths are those in which we not only learn that the proposition *is* true, but see that it *must be* true; in which the negation of the truth is not only false, but impossible; in which we cannot, even by an effort of imagination, or in a supposition, conceive the reverse of that which is asserted. That there are such truths cannot be doubted. We may take, for example, all relations of number. Three and Two added together make Five. We cannot conceive it to be otherwise. We cannot, by any freak of thought, imagine Three and Two to make Seven."[4]

Although Dr. Whewell has naturally and properly employed a variety of phrases to bring his meaning more forcibly home, he would, I presume, allow that they are all equivalent; and that what he means by a necessary truth, would be sufficiently defined, a proposition the negation of which is not only false but inconceivable. I am unable to find in any of his expressions, turn them what way you will, a meaning beyond this, and I do not believe he would contend that they mean anything more.

This, therefore, is the principle asserted: that propositions, the negation of which is inconceivable, or in other words, which we cannot figure to ourselves as being false, must rest on evidence of a higher and more cogent description than any which experience can afford.

Now I cannot but wonder that so much stress should be laid on the circumstance of inconceivableness, when there is such

[2] *History of Scientific Ideas*, i. 65–67.
[3] Ibid., i. 60.
[4] Ibid. 58, 59.

ample experience to show that our capacity or incapacity of conceiving a thing has very little to do with the possibility of the thing in itself; but is in truth very much an affair of accident, and depends on the past history and habits of our own minds. There is no more generally acknowledged fact in human nature, than the extreme difficulty at first felt in conceiving anything as possible, which is in contradiction to long established and familiar experience; or even to old familiar habits of thought. And this difficulty is a necessary result of the fundamental laws of the human mind. When we have often seen and thought of two things together, and have never in any one instance either seen or thought of them separately, there is by the primary law of association an increasing difficulty, which may in the end become insuperable, of conceiving the two things apart. This is most of all conspicuous in uneducated persons, who are in general utterly unable to separate any two ideas which have once become firmly associated in their minds; and if persons of cultivated intellect have any advantage on the point, it is only because, having seen and heard and read more, and being more accustomed to exercise their imagination, they have experienced their sensations and thoughts in more varied combinations, and have been prevented from forming many of these inseparable associations. But this advantage has necessarily its limits. The most practised intellect is not exempt from the universal laws of our conceptive faculty. If daily habit presents to any one for a long period two facts in combination, and if he is not led during that period either by accident or by his voluntary mental operations to think of them apart, he will probably in time become incapable of doing so even by the strongest effort; and the supposition that the two facts can be separated in nature, will at last present itself to his mind with all the characters of an inconceivable phenomenon.[5] There are remarkable instances of this in the history of science: instances in which the most instructed men rejected as impossible, because inconceivable, things which their posterity, by earlier practice and longer perseverance in the attempt, found it quite easy to conceive, and which everybody now knows to be true. There

---

[5] "If all mankind had spoken one language, we cannot doubt that there would have been a powerful, perhaps a universal, school of philosophers, who would have believed in the inherent connexion between names and things, who would have taken the sound *man* to be the mode of agitating the air which is essentially communicative of the ideas of reason, cookery, bipedality, &c."—De Morgan, *Formal Logic*, p. 246.

was a time when men of the most cultivated intellects, and the most emancipated from the dominion of early prejudice, could not credit the existence of antipodes; were unable to conceive, in opposition to old association, the force of gravity acting upwards instead of downwards. The Cartesians long rejected the Newtonian doctrine of the gravitation of all bodies towards one another, on the faith of a general proposition, the reverse of which seemed to them to be inconceivable—the proposition that a body cannot act where it is not. All the cumbrous machinery of imaginary vortices, assumed without the smallest particle of evidence, appeared to these philosophers a more rational mode of explaining the heavenly motions, than one which involved what seemed to them so great an absurdity. And they no doubt found it as impossible to conceive that a body should act upon the earth from the distance of the sun or moon, as we find it to conceive an end to space or time, or two straight lines inclosing a space. Newton himself had not been able to realize the conception, or we should not have had his hypothesis of a subtle ether, the occult cause of gravitation; and his writings prove, that though he deemed the particular nature of the intermediate agency a matter of conjecture, the necessity of *some* such agency appeared to him indubitable.

If, then, it be so natural to the human mind, even in a high state of culture, to be incapable of conceiving, and on that ground to believe impossible, what is afterwards not only found to be conceivable but proved to be true; what wonder if in cases where the association is still older, more confirmed, and more familiar, and in which nothing ever occurs to shake our conviction, or even suggest to us any conception at variance with the association, the acquired incapacity should continue, and be mistaken for a natural incapacity? It is true, our experience of the varieties in nature enables us, within certain limits, to conceive the sun or moon falling; for though we never saw them fall, nor ever perhaps imagined them falling, we have seen so many other things fall, that we have innumerable familiar analogies to assist the conception; which, after all, we should probably have some difficulty in framing, were we not well accustomed to see the sun and moon move (or appear to move,) so that we are only called upon to conceive a slight change in the direction of motion, a circumstance familiar to our experience. But when experience affords no model on which to shape the new conception, how is it possible for us to form it? How, for example, can we imagine an end to space or time? We never saw any object without something beyond it, nor experienced any feeling without something following it. When, therefore, we attempt to conceive the last point of space, we have the idea irresistibly raised of other points beyond it. When we try to imagine the last instant of time, we cannot help conceiving another instant after it. Nor is there any necessity to assume, as is done by a modern school of metaphysicians, a peculiar fundamental law of the mind to account for the feeling of infinity inherent in our conceptions of space and time; that apparent infinity is sufficiently accounted for by simpler and universally acknowledged laws.

Now, in the case of a geometrical axiom, such, for example, as that two straight lines cannot inclose a space,—a truth which is testified to us by our very earliest impressions of the external world,—how is it possible (whether those external impressions be or be not the ground of our belief) that the reverse of the proposition *could* be otherwise than inconceivable to us? What analogy have we, what similar order of facts in any other branch of our experience, to facilitate to us the conception of two straight lines inclosing a space? Nor is even this all. I have already called attention to the peculiar property of our impressions of form, that the ideas or mental images exactly resemble their prototypes, and adequately represent them for the purposes of scientific observation. From this, and from the intuitive character of the observation, which in this case reduces itself to simple inspection, we cannot so much as call up in our imagination two straight lines, in order to attempt to conceive them inclosing a space, without by that very act repeating the scientific experiment which establishes the contrary. Will it really be contended that the inconceivableness of the thing, in such circumstances, proves anything against the experimental origin of the conviction? Is it not clear that in whichever mode our belief in the proposition may have originated, the impossibility of our conceiving the negative of it must, on either hypothesis, be the same? As, then, Dr. Whewell exhorts those who have any difficulty in recognising the distinction held by him between necessary and contingent truths, to study geometry,—a condition which I can assure him I have conscientiously fulfilled,—I, in return, with equal confidence, exhort those who agree with him, to study the general laws of association; being convinced that nothing more is requisite than a moderate familiarity with those laws, to dispel the illusion which ascribes a peculiar necessity to our earliest inductions from experience, and measures the possibility of things in themselves, by the human capacity of conceiving them.

I hope to be pardoned for adding, that Dr. Whewell himself has both confirmed by his testimony the effect of habitual association in giving to an experimental truth the appearance of a necessary one, and afforded a striking instance of that remarkable law in his own person. In his *Philosophy of the Inductive Sciences* he continually asserts, that propositions which not only are not self-evident, but which we know to have been discovered gradually, and by great efforts of genius and patience, have, when once established, appeared so self-evident that, but for historical proof, it would have been impossible to conceive that they had not been recognised from the first by all persons in a sound state of their faculties. "We now despise those who, in the Copernican controversy, could not conceive the apparent motion of the sun on the heliocentric hypothesis; or those who, in opposition to Galileo, thought that a uniform force might be that which generated a velocity proportional to the space; or those who held there was something absurd in Newton's doctrine of the different refrangibility of different coloured rays; or those who imagined that when elements combine, their sensible qualities must be manifest in the compound; or those who were reluctant to give up the distinction of vegetables into herbs, shrubs, and trees. We cannot help thinking that men must have been singularly dull of comprehension, to find a difficulty in admitting what is to us so plain and simple. We have a latent persuasion that we in their place should have been wiser and more clear-sighted; that we should have taken the right side, and given our assent at once to the truth. Yet in reality such a persuasion is a mere delusion. The person who, in such instances as the above, were on the losing side, were very far, in most cases, from being persons more prejudiced, or stupid, or narrow-minded, than the greater part of mankind now are; and the cause for which they fought was far from being a manifestly bad one, till it had been so decided by the result of the war. . . . So complete has been the victory of truth in most of these instances, that at present we can hardly imagine the struggle to have been necessary. *The very essence of these triumphs is, that they lead us to regard the views we reject as not only false but inconceivable.*"[6]

[6] *Novum Organum Renovatum*, pp. 32, 33.

This last proposition is precisely what I contend for; and I ask no more, in order to overthrow the whole theory of its author on the nature of the evidence of axioms. For what is that theory? That the truth of axioms cannot have been learnt from experience, because their falsity is inconceivable. But Dr. Whewell himself says, that we are continually led, by the natural progress of thought, to regard as inconceivable what our forefathers not only conceived but believed, nay even (he might have added) were unable to conceive the reverse of. He cannot intend to justify this mode of thought: he cannot mean to say, that we can be right in regarding as inconceivable what others have conceived, and as self-evident what to others did not appear evident at all. After so complete an admission that inconceivableness is an accidental thing, not inherent in the phenomenon itself, but dependent on the mental history of the person who tries to conceive it, how can he ever call upon us to reject a proposition as impossible on no other ground than its inconceivableness? Yet he not only does so, but has unintentionally afforded some of the most remarkable examples which can be cited of the very illusion which he has himself so clearly pointed out. I select as specimens, his remarks on the evidence of the three laws of motion, and of the atomic theory.

With respect to the laws of motion, Dr. Whewell says: "No one can doubt that, in historical fact, these laws were collected from experience. That such is the case, is no matter of conjecture. We know the time, the persons, the circumstances, belonging to each step of each discovery."[7] After this testimony, to adduce evidence of the fact would be superfluous. And not only were these laws by no means intuitively evident, but some of them were originally paradoxes. The first law was especially so. That a body, once in motion, would continue for ever to move in the same direction with undiminished velocity unless acted upon by some new force, was a proposition which mankind found for a long time the greatest difficulty in crediting. It stood opposed to apparent experience of the most familiar kind, which taught that it was the nature of motion to abate gradually, and at last terminate of itself. Yet when once the contrary doctrine was firmly established, mathematicians, as Dr. Whewell observes, speedily began to believe that laws, thus contradictory to first appearances, and which, even after full proof had been obtained, it

[7] *History of Scientific Ideas*, i. 264.

had required generations to render familiar to the minds of the scientific world, were under a "demonstrable necessity, compelling them to be such as they are and no other;" and he himself, though not venturing "absolutely to pronounce" that *all* these laws "can be rigorously traced to an absolute necessity in the nature of things,"[8] does actually so think of the law just mentioned; of which he says: "Though the discovery of the first law of motion was made, historically speaking, by means of experiment, we have now attained a point of view in which we see that it might have been certainly known to be true, independently of experience."[9] Can there be a more striking exemplification than is here afforded, of the effect of association which we have described? Philosophers, for generations, have the most extraordinary difficulty in putting certain ideas together; they at last succeed in doing so; and after a sufficient repetition of the process, they first fancy a natural bond between the ideas, then experience a growing difficulty, which at last, by the continuation of the same progress, becomes an impossibility, of severing them from one another. If such be the progress of an experimental conviction of which the date is of yesterday, and which is in opposition to first appearances, how must it fare with those which are conformable to appearances familiar from the first dawn of intelligence, and of the conclusiveness of which, from the earliest records of human thought, no sceptic has suggested even a momentary doubt?

The other instance which I shall quote is a truly astonishing one, and may be called the *reductio ad absurdum* of the theory of inconceivableness. Speaking of the laws of chemical composition, Dr. Whewell says:[10] "That they could never have been clearly understood, and therefore never firmly established, without laborious and exact experiments, is certain; but yet we may venture to say, that being once known, they possess an evidence beyond that of mere experiment. *For how in fact can we conceive combinations, otherwise than as definite in kind and quality?* If we were to suppose each element ready to combine with any other indifferently, and indifferently in any quantity, we should have a world in which all would be confusion and indefiniteness. There would be no fixed kinds of bodies. Salts, and stones, and ores, would approach to

8 *Hist. Sc. Id.,* i. 263.
9 Ibid. 240.
10 Ibid. ii. 25, 26.

and graduate into each other by insensible degrees. Instead of this, we know that the world consists of bodies distinguishable from each other by definite differences, capable of being classified and named, and of having general propositions asserted concerning them. And as *we cannot conceive a world in which this should not be the case,* it would appear that we cannot conceive a state of things in which the laws of the combination of elements should not be of that definite and measured kind which we have above asserted."

That a philosopher of Dr. Whewell's eminence should gravely assert that we cannot conceive a world in which the simple elements should combine in other than definite proportions; that by dint of meditating on a scientific truth, the original discoverer of which was still living, he should have rendered the association in his own mind between the idea of combination and that of constant proportions so familiar and intimate as to be unable to conceive the one fact without the other; is so signal an instance of the mental law for which I am contending, that one word more in illustration must be superfluous.

In the latest and most complete elaboration of his metaphysical system (the *Philosophy of Discovery*), as well as in the earlier discourse on the *Fundamental Antithesis of Philosophy,* reprinted as an appendix to that work, Dr. Whewell, while very candidly admitting that his language was open to misconception, disclaims having intended to say that mankind in general can *now* perceive the law of definite proportions in chemical combination to be a necessary truth. All he meant was that philosophical chemists in a future generation may possibly see this. "Some truths may be seen by intuition, but yet the intuition of them may be a rare and a difficult attainment."[11] And he explains that the inconceivableness which, according to his theory, is the test of axioms, "depends entirely upon the clearness of the Ideas which the axioms involve. So long as those ideas are vague and indistinct, the contrary of an axiom may be assented to, though it cannot be distinctly conceived. It may be assented to, not because it is possible, but because we do not see clearly what is possible. To a person who is only beginning to think geometrically, there may appear nothing absurd in the assertion, that two straight lines may inclose a space. And in the same manner, to a person who is only beginning to think of mechanical truths, it may not appear to be absurd, that in mechanical processes,

[11] *Phil. of Disc.*, p. 339.

Reaction should be greater or less than Action; and so, again, to a person who has not thought steadily about Substance, it may not appear inconceivable, that by chemical operations, we should generate new matter, or destroy matter which already exists."[12] Necessary truths, therefore, are not those of which we cannot conceive, but "those of which we cannot *distinctly* conceive the contrary."[13] So long as our ideas are indistinct altogether, we do not know what is or is not capable of being distinctly conceived; but, by the ever increasing distinctness with which scientific men apprehend the general conceptions of science, they in time come to perceive that there are certain laws of nature, which, though historically and as a matter of fact they were learnt from experience, we cannot, now that we know them, distinctly conceive to be other than they are.

The account which I should give of this progress of the scientific mind is somewhat different. After a general law of nature has been ascertained, men's minds do not at first acquire a complete facility of familiarly representing to themselves the phenomena of nature in the character which that law assigns to them. The habit which constitutes the scientific cast of mind, that of conceiving facts of all descriptions conformably to the laws which regulate them—phenomena of all descriptions according to the relations which have been ascertained really to exist between them; this habit, in the case of newly discovered relations, comes only by degrees. So long as it is not thoroughly formed, no necessary character is ascribed to the new truth. But in time the philosopher attains a state of mind in which his mental picture of nature spontaneously represents to him all the phenomena with which the new theory is concerned, in the exact light in which the theory regards them: all images or conceptions derived from any other theory, or from the confused view of the facts which is anterior to any theory, having entirely disappeared from his mind. The mode of representing facts which results from the theory, has now become, to his faculties, the only natural mode of conceiving them. It is a known truth, that a prolonged habit of arranging phenomena in certain groups, and explaining them by means of certain principles, makes any other arrangement or explanation of these facts be felt as unnatural: and it may at last become as difficult to him to represent the

[12] Ibid. p. 338.
[13] Ibid. p. 463.

facts to himself in any other mode, as it often was, originally, to represent them in that mode.

But, further, (if the theory is true, as we are supposing it to be,) any other mode in which he tries, or in which he was formerly accustomed, to represent the phenomena, will be seen by him to be inconsistent with the facts that suggested the new theory—facts which now form a part of his mental picture of nature. And since a contradiction is always inconceivable, his imagination rejects these false theories, and declares itself incapable of conceiving them. Their inconceivableness to him does not, however, result from anything in the theories themselves, intrinsically and à *priori* repugnant to the human faculties; it results from the repugnance between them and a portion of the facts; which facts as long as he did not know, or did not distinctly realize in his mental representations, the false theory did not appear other than conceivable; it becomes inconceivable, merely from the fact that contradictory elements cannot be combined in the same conception. Although, then, his real reason for rejecting theories at variance with the true one, is no other than that they clash with his experience, he easily falls into the belief, that he rejects them because they are inconceivable, and that he adopts the true theory because it is self-evident, and does not need the evidence of experience at all. . . .

In the examination which formed the subject of the last chapter, into the nature of the evidence of those deductive sciences which are commonly represented to be systems of necessary truth, we have been led to the following conclusions. The results of those sciences are indeed necessary, In the sense of necessarily following from certain first principles, commonly called axioms and definitions; that is, of being certainly true if those axioms and definitions are so; for the word necessity, even in this acceptation of it, means no more than certainty. But their claim to the character of necessity in any sense beyond this, as implying an evidence independent of and superior to observation and experience, must depend on the previous establishment of such a claim in favour of the definitions and axioms themselves. With regard to axioms, we found that, considered as experimental truths, they rest on superabundant and obvious evidence. We inquired whether, since this is the case, it be imperative to suppose any other evidence of those truths than experimental evidence, any other origin for our belief of them than an experimental origin. We decided, that the burden of proof lies with those who maintain the affirmative, and we examined, at considerable length, such arguments as they have produced. The examination having led to the rejection of those arguments, we have thought ourselves warranted in concluding that axioms are but a class, the most universal class, of inductions from experience; the simplest and easiest cases of generalization from the facts furnished to us by our senses or by our internal consciousness.

While the axioms of demonstrative sciences thus appeared to be experimental truths, the definitions, as they are incorrectly called, in those sciences, were found by us to be generalizations from experience which are not even, accurately speaking, truths; being propositions in which, while we assert of some kind of object, some property or properties which observation shows to belong to it, we at the same time deny that it possesses any other properties, though in truth other properties do in every individual instance accompany, and in almost all instances modify, the property thus exclusively predicated. The denial, therefore, is a mere fiction, or supposition, made for the purpose of excluding the consideration of those modifying circumstances, when their influence is of too trifling amount to be worth considering, or adjourning it, when important, to a more convenient moment.

From these considerations it would appear that Deductive or Demonstrative Sciences are all, without exception, Inductive Sciences; that their evidence is that of experience; but that they are also, in virtue of the peculiar character of one indispensable portion of the general formulæ according to which their inductions are made, Hypothetical Sciences. Their conclusions are only true on certain suppositions, which are, or ought to be, approximations to the truth, but are seldom, if ever, exactly true; and to this hypothetical character is to be ascribed the peculiar certainty, which is supposed to be inherent in demonstration.

What we have now asserted, however, cannot be received as universally true of Deductive or Demonstrative Sciences, until verified by being applied to the most remarkable of all those sciences, that of Numbers; the theory of the Calculus; Arithmetic and Algebra. It is harder to believe of the doctrines of this science than of any other, either that they are not truths à *priori,* but experimental truths, or that their peculiar certainty is owing to their being not absolute but only conditional truths. This, therefore, is a case which merits examination apart; and the more so, because on this subject we have a double set of doctrines to contend with; that of the à *priori* philosophers on one side; and on the other, a theory the most opposite to theirs, which was at one time very generally received, and is still far from being altogether exploded, among metaphysicians.

This theory attempts to solve the difficulty apparently inherent in the case, by representing the propositions of the science of numbers as merely verbal, and its processes as simple transformations of language, substitutions of one expression for another. The proposition, Two and one is equal to three; a statement that mankind have agreed to use the name assertion of a really existing fact, but a definition of the word three; a statement that mankind have agreed to use the name three as a sign exactly equivalent to two and one; to call by the former name whatever is called by the other more clumsy phrase. According to this doctrine the longest process in algebra is but a succession of changes in terminology, by which equivalent expressions are substituted one for another; a series of translations of the same fact, from one into another language; though how, after such a series of translations, the fact itself comes out changed (as when we demonstrate a new geometrical theorem by algebra), they have not explained; and it is a difficulty which is fatal to their theory.

It must be acknowledged that there are peculiarities in the processes of arithmetic and algebra which render the theory in question very plausible, and have not unnaturally made those sciences the stronghold of Nominalism. The doctrine that we can discover facts, detect the hidden processes of nature, by an artful manipulation of language, is so contrary to common sense, that a person must have made some advances in philosophy to believe it; men fly to so paradoxical a belief to avoid, as they think, some even greater difficulty, which the vulgar do not see. What has led many to believe that reasoning is a mere verbal process, is, that no other theory seemed reconcileable with the nature of the Science of Numbers. For we do not carry any ideas along with us when we use the symbols of arithmetic or of algebra. In a geometrical demonstration we have a mental diagram, if not one on paper; AB, AC, are present to our imagination as lines, intersecting other lines, forming an angle with one another, and the like; but not so a and b. These may represent lines or any other magnitudes, but those magnitudes are never thought of; nothing is realized in our imagination but a and b. The ideas which, on the particular occasion, they happen to represent, are banished from the mind during every intermediate part of the process, between the beginning, when the premises are translated from things into signs, and the end, when the conclusion is translated back from signs into things. Nothing, then, being in the reasoner's mind but the symbols, what can seem more inadmissible than to contend that the reasoning process has to do with anything more? We seem to have come to one of Bacon's Prerogative Instances; an *experimentum crucis* on the nature of reasoning itself.

Nevertheless, it will appear on consideration, that this apparently so decisive instance is no instance at all; that there is in every step of an arithmetical or algebraical calculation a real induction, a real inference of facts from facts; and that what disguises the induction is simply its comprehensive nature and the consequent extreme generality of the language. All numbers must be numbers of something; there are no such things as numbers in the abstract. *Ten* must mean ten bodies, or ten sounds, or ten beatings of the pulse. But though numbers must be numbers of something, they may be numbers of anything. Propositions, therefore, concerning numbers, have the remarkable peculiarity that they are propositions concerning all things whatever; all objects, all existences of every kind, known to our experience. All things possess quantity; consist of parts which can be numbered; and in that character possess all the properties which are called properties of numbers. That half of four is two, must be true whatever the word four represents, whether four hours, four miles, or four pounds weight. We need only conceive a thing divided into four equal parts (and all things may be conceived as so divided), to be able to predicate of it every property of the number four, that is, every arithmetical proposition in which the number four stands on one side of the equation. Algebra extends the generalization still farther: every number represents that particular number of all things without distinction, but every algebraical symbol does more, it represents all numbers without distinction. As soon as we conceive a thing divided into equal parts, without knowing into what number of parts, we may call it a or x, and apply to it, without danger of error, every algebraical formula in the books. The proposition, $2(a + b) = 2a + 2b$, is a truth co-extensive with all nature. Since then algebraical truths are true of all things whatever, and not, like those of geometry, true of lines only or of angles only, it is no wonder that the symbols should not excite in our minds ideas of any things in particular. When we demonstrate the forty-seventh proposition of Euclid, it is not necessary that the words should raise in us an image of all right-angled triangles, but only of some one right-angled triangle; so in algebra we need not, under the symbol a, picture to ourselves all things whatever, but only some one thing; why not, then, the letter itself? The mere written characters, a, b, x, y, z, serve as well for representatives of Things in general, as any more complex and apparently more concrete conception. That we are conscious of them however in their character of things, and not of mere signs, is evident from the fact that our whole process of reasoning is carried on by predicating of them the properties of things. In resolving an algebraic equation, by what rules do we proceed? By applying at each step to a, b, and x, the proposition that equals added to equals make equals; that equals taken from equals leave equals; and other propositions founded on these two. These are not properties of language, or of signs as such, but of magnitudes, which is as much as to say, of all things. The inferences, therefore, which are successively drawn, are inferences concerning things, not symbols; though as any Things whatever will serve the turn, there is no necessity for keeping the idea of the Thing at all distinct, and consequently the process of thought may, in this case, be allowed without danger to do what all processes of thought, when they have been performed often, will do if permitted, namely, to become entirely mechanical. Hence the general language of algebra comes to be used familiarly without exciting ideas, as all other general language is prone to do from mere habit, though in no other case than this can it be done with complete safety. But when we look back to see from whence the probative force of the process is derived, we find that at every single step, unless we suppose ourselves to be thinking and talking of the things, and not the mere symbols, the evidence fails.

There is another circumstance, which, still more than that which we have now mentioned, gives plausibility to the notion that the propositions of arithmetic and algebra are merely verbal. That is, that when considered as propositions respecting Things, they all have the appearance of being identical propositions. The assertion, Two and one is equal to three, considered as an assertion respecting objects, as for instance "Two pebbles and one pebble are equal to three pebbles," does not affirm equality between two collections of pebbles, but absolute identity. It affirms that if we put one pebble to two pebbles, those very pebbles are three. The objects, therefore, being the very same, and the mere assertion that "objects are themselves" being insignificant, it seems but natural to consider the proposition Two and one is equal to three, as asserting mere identity of signification between the two names.

This, however, though it looks so plausible, will not bear examination. The expression "two pebbles and one pebble," and the expression, "three pebbles," stand indeed for the same aggregation of objects, but they by no means stand for the same physical fact. They are names of the same objects, but of those objects in two different states: though they *de*note the same things, their *con*notation is different. Three pebbles in two separate parcels, and three pebbles in one parcel, do not make the same impression on our senses; and the assertion that the very same pebbles may by an alteration of place and arrangement be made to produce either the one set of sensations or the other, though a very familiar proposition, is not an identical one. It is a truth known to us by early and constant experience: an inductive truth; and such truths are the foundation of the science of Number. The fundamental truths of that science all rest on the evidence of sense; they are proved by showing to our eyes and our fingers that any given number of objects, ten balls for example, may by separation and re-arrangement exhibit to our senses all the different sets of numbers the sum of which is equal to ten. All the improved methods of teaching arithmetic to children proceed on a knowledge of this fact. All who wish to carry the child's *mind* along with them in learning arithmetic; all who wish to teach numbers, and not mere ciphers—now teach it through the evidence of the senses, in the manner we have described.

We may, if we please, call the proposition, "Three is two and one," a definition of the number three, and assert that arithmetic, as it has been asserted that geometry, is a science founded on definitions. But they are definitions in the geometrical sense, not the logical; asserting not the meaning of a term only, but along with it an observed matter of fact. The proposition, "A circle is a figure bounded by a line which has all its points equally distant from a point within it," is called the definition of a circle; but the proposition from which so many consequences follow, and which is really a first principle in geometry, is, that figures answering to this description exist. And thus we may call "Three is two and one" a definition of three; but the calculations which depend on that proposition do not follow from the definition itself, but from an arithmetical theorem presupposed on it, namely, that collections of objects exist, which while they impress the senses thus, °₀°, may be separated into two parts, thus, oo o. This proposition being granted, we term all such parcels Threes, after which the enunciation of the above mentioned physical fact will serve also for a definition of the word Three.

The Science of Numbers is thus no exception to the conclusion we previously arrived at, that the processes even of deductive sciences are altogether inductive, and that their first principles are generalisations from experience. It remains to be examined whether this science resembles geometry in the further circumstance, that some of its inductions are not exactly true; and that the peculiar certainty ascribed to it, on account of which its propositions are called necessary Truths, is fictitious and hypothetical, being true in no other sense than that those propositions legitimately follow from the hypothesis of the truth of premises which are avowedly mere approximations to truth. . . .

Gottlob Frege
(1848–1925)

Views of Some
Writers on the Nature
of Arithmetical
Propositions

74 *In this selection Frege examines the views of Kant, Leibniz,
and Mill on the nature of such propositions as 7+5=12 and
finds the views of all three wanting. It should be borne in mind,
however, that mathematical propositions are only a part of a
large group of propositions whose nature raises problems for
philosophy. However successful Frege's attacks on these authors' views of the nature of mathematics, their views on the
other problematic propositions are not thereby shown faulty.*

One must distinguish those numerical formulae, such as $2+3=5$, which deal with particular numbers, from the general
laws which hold true for all whole numbers.

Some philosophers[1] consider the former to be unprovable
and immediately evident like axioms. Kant[2] declares them to be
unprovable and synthetic but is loath to call them axioms because they are not general and because they are infinite in
number. Hankel[3] justifiably calls this assumption of infinitely
many unprovable primitive truths inappropriate and paradoxical. It does indeed conflict with the intellect's need for the
perspicuity of first principles. And is it really self-evident that

$$135664+37863=173527?$$

No! and yet it is precisely this that Kant adduces in support of
the position that these propositions are synthetic in nature.

From Gottlob Frege, *Die Grundlagen der Arithmetik*, Sections 5–10.
Breslau: Wilhelm Koebner, 1884. Translation especially for this volume by
Eike-Henner Kluge.

[1] Hobbes, Locke, Newton. Cf. Baumann, *Die Lehren von Zeit, Raum und
Mathematik* (Berlin, 1868) Vol. I, pp. 241 and 242.

[2] *Critique of Pure Reason;* collected works edited by Hartenstein, Vol. III,
p. 157 (A164/B205).

[3] *Vorlesungen über die komplexen Zahlen und ihre Functionen*, p. 55.

But it tells rather against their unprovability; for how else are they to be understood if not by means of a proof, seeing that they are not immediately evident? Kant wants to make use of an intuition of fingers or points, whereby he runs the risk of making the propositions appear to be empirical, contrary to his own opinion; for no matter what, an intuition of 37863 fingers is certainly not a pure one. Neither does the expression "intuition" seem to be quite appropriate, since even 10 fingers, in virtue of their positions with respect to one another, can give rise to the most diverse intuitions. And do we really have an intuition of 135664 fingers or points? If we did have one, and likewise one of 37863 fingers and one of 173527 fingers, then the correctness of our equation, if it were not provable, would be immediately evident, at least so far as fingers are concerned; but this is not the case.

Kant obviously had only small numbers in mind, so that those formulae which would be provable for large numbers would be immediately evident by means of intuition in the case of small numbers. But it is awkward to make a fundamental distinction between small and large numbers, particularly since it might not be possible to draw a sharp boundary. If the numerical formulae from, say, 10 on were provable, one would justifiably ask, "Why not from 5 on? from 2 on? from 1 on?"

Other philosophers and mathematicians have in fact maintained the provability of numerical formulae. Leibniz says,[4]

It is not an immediate truth that 2 and 2 are 4, it being presupposed that 4 signifies 3 and 1. One can prove it, namely thus:

Definitions: *1. 2 is 1 and 1.*
2. 3 is 2 and 1.
3. 4 is 3 and 1.

Axiom: *If equals are substituted for equals, the equality remains.*
Proof: 2+2=(Def. 1)2+1+1=(Def. 2)3+1=(Def. 3)4
Therefore: 2+2=4 by the axiom.

At first, this proof seems to be constructed entirely out of the definitions and the axiom cited. This last, too, could be transformed into a definition, as Leibniz himself did in another pas-

---

4 *Nouveaux Essais*, IV, 10. Erdmann edition, p. 363.

sage.[5] It seems that one needs to know no more of 1, 2, 3, 4 than is contained in the definitions. Upon closer examination, however, one discovers a gap (in the proof) which is concealed by the omission of the brackets. For, to be more accurate, it ought to be written

$$2+2=2+(1+1)$$
$$(2+1)+1=3+1=4$$

What is here missing is the proposition

$$2+(1+1)=(2+1)+1$$

which is a special case of

$$a+(b+c)=(a+b)+c.$$

If one assumes this law, one can easily see that every formula of addition can be proved in this way. Every number is then to be defined in terms of its predecessor. As a matter of fact, I don't see how, say, the number 437986 could be given to us more appropriately than in Leibniz's way. In this way we still acquire command of it, even without having an intuition of it. Through such definitions the infinite set of numbers is reduced to one and increment by one, and each of the infinitely many formulae can be proved from a few general propositions.

This opinion is also shared by H. Grasmann and H. Hankel. The former wants to obtain the law

$$a+(b+1)=(a+b)+1$$

by means of a definition in that he says

If a and b are any arbitrary members of the basic series, then by the sum a + b *we understand that number of the basic series for which the formula*

$$a+(b+e)=a+b+e$$

is valid.[6]

e is here supposed to refer to the positive number one. This explanation can be criticized in two different ways. First, sum is explained in terms of itself. If one does not yet know what a + b is supposed to mean, then one does not understand the expression a + (b +e) either. But perhaps this objection can be met by saying, admittedly in contradiction to the precise

[5] Non inelegans specimen demonstrandi in abstractis. (Erdmann edition, p. 94).
[6] *Lehrbuch der Mathematik für höhere Lehranstalten,* part I: Arithmetik; (Stettin, 1860) p. 4.

wording, that what is supposed to be explained is not sum but addition. In that case, it could still be objected that if there were either none or several members of the basic series which were of the requisite sort, then $a + b$ would be an empty sign. Grassmann simply assumes and does not prove that this does not occur; so that the rigor is only apparent.

One should have thought that numerical formulae are synthetic or analytic, *a posteriori* or *a priori,* depending on whether the general laws on which their proof depends are so. John Stuart Mill, however, is of the opposite opinion. To be sure, initially he seems to want to base the science on definitions,[7] as does Leibniz; but this correct thought is immediately spoiled by his preconception of all knowledge as empirical. For, so he enlightens us,[8] these definitions are not definitions in any logical sense; they not only stipulate the meaning of an expression but in so doing also assert an observed matter of fact. What in the world could be this observed, or as Mill also puts it, this physical fact which is asserted in the definition of the number 777864? Of the entire wealth of physical facts which here opens up before us, Mill names only a single one, which is supposed to be asserted in the definition of the number 3. According to him, it consists in the fact that there are combinations of objects which, while they impress the sense thus $^\circ{}_\circ{}^\circ$, can be divided into two parts, thus: $\circ\circ\,\circ$. Thank heaven that not everything in the world is fixed and immovable, else we could not undertake this separation, and $2 + 1$ would not be 3! What a pity that Mill did not also illustrate the physical facts underlying the numbers 0 and 1!

Mill continues, "This proposition being granted, we call all such units 3." From this we see that really it is incorrect to speak of three strokes when the clock strikes three, or to call sweet, sour and bitter three sensations of taste; and the expression "three methods of solving an equation" is equally as inadmissable, for from none of the foregoing do we ever get the same impression as from $^\circ{}_\circ{}^\circ$.

Now Mill states, "The calculations do not follow from the definition itself, but from the observed fact." But at what point in the above proof of the proposition $2+2=4$ ought Leibniz to have appealed to the fact in question? Mill neglects to indicate the gap, although he does give a proof of the proposi-

[7] System of Logic, Bk. III, chap. xxix, § 5 (German translation by J. Schiel).

[8] Op. cit. Bk. II, chap. vi, § 2.

tion $5+2=7^9$ which wholly corresponds to the one given by Leibniz. The gap which actually does exist—consisting in the omission of the brackets—he overlooks, just as does Leibniz.

If the definition of every single number really did assert a particular matter of fact, then one could never admire enough for his knowledge of physical facts the man who calculates with nine-figure numbers. However, perhaps Mill's opinion does not go so far as to require that all these facts have to be observed separately, but that it suffices to have derived, by means of induction, a general law in which they are included together. But try to enunciate this law, and it will be found to be impossible. It does not suffice to say that there are large collections of things which can be divided; for this does not mean that there are such large collections and of the sort necessary for the definition of, say, the number 1,000,000; nor is the manner of division specified any more precisely. Mill's view necessarily leads to the demand that a fact should be observed specially for each number, since it is precisely this peculiarity of the number 1,000,000 which necessarily belongs to its definition, that would be lost in a general law. According to Mill, one ought not in fact posit 1,000,000=999,-999+1 unless one had observed precisely this particular way of dividing a collection of things, where this manner of division is distinct from that belonging to any other number.

Mill seems to think that the definitions 2=1+1, 3=2+1, 4=3+1, etc, ought not to be formed until the facts mentioned by him have been observed. To be sure, one ought not to define 3 as (2+1) if one attaches no sense at all to (2+1). But the question is whether for this it is necessary to observe this collection and its division. If it were, then the number 0 would be puzzling; for as yet no one, surely, has seen or touched 0 pebbles. Mill would of course declare 0 to be something senseless, a mere turn of speech; calculations with 0 would be a mere game with empty signs, and it would be a wonder indeed how something rational could come of it. However, if these calculations do have a serious meaning, then neither can the sign 0 itself be completely senseless. And the possibility suggests itself that 2+1, in a way similar to 0, could still have a sense even if the fact mentioned by Mill were not observed. Who would want to claim that the fact which according to Mill is contained in an 18-figure number has ever

---

[9] Op. cit., Bk. III, chap. XXIV, § 5.

been observed; and who would want to deny that such a number-sign nevertheless does have a sense?

One may perhaps think that physical facts would be needed only for the smaller numbers, say up to 10; whereas the remaining ones could be constructed out of these. However, if one can form 11 out of 10 and 1 simply by means of a definition, without having seen the corresponding collection, then there is no reason why one cannot also form 2 out of 1 and 1 in the same way. If calculations with the number 11 do not follow from the matter of fact which is characteristic for that number, how does it happen that calculations with 2 must be based on the observation of a certain collection and the division peculiar to it?

One may perhaps ask how arithmetic could exist if we could distinguish nothing whatever by means of our senses, or at most three things. Surely such a state of affairs would have been somewhat awkward for our knowledge of arithmetical propositions and their applications; but would it also affect their truth? If one calls a proposition empirical because we must have made observations in order to become aware of its content, then one is not using the word "empirical" in a sense which is opposed to that of "a priori." One is stating a psychological claim which concerns the content of the proposition alone; whether it is true is here a matter of no concern. In that sense, all of Münchhausen's stories, too, are empirical; for certainly one must have observed all sorts of things in order to be able to invent them.

Are the Laws of Arithmetic Inductive Truths?

The preceding considerations make it probable that numerical formulae are derivable solely from the definitions of the particular numbers by means of a few general laws, and that the definitions in order to be legitimate neither assert observed facts nor presuppose them. The important thing, therefore, is to understand the nature of these laws.

For his proof of the formula 5+2=7, which was mentioned above, Mill[10] wants to make use of the proposition "Whatever is constituted of parts, is constituted of the parts of these parts." This he takes to be a more characteristic expression

[10] Op. cit., Bk. III, chap. XXIV, § 5.

of the proposition which is more familiar in the form "Sums of equals are equals." He calls it an inductive truth, and a law of nature of the highest order. It is indicative of the inexactitude of his presentation that when he comes to the point in the proof where, according to his opinion, this proposition is indispensible, he does not even adduce it; however, it seems that his inductive truth is supposed to replace Leibniz's axiom, "If equals are substituted for equals, the equality remains." But in order to be able to call arithmetical truths laws of nature, Mill gives them a sense which they do not have. For example,[11] he thinks that the equation $1=1$ could be false because one pound-weight does not always have precisely the same weight as another. But the proposition $1=1$ does not want to say that at all.

Mill understands the sign $+$ in such a way that by means of it is expressed the relation of the parts of a physical body or heap to the whole; but that is not the sense of this sign. $5+2=7$ does not mean that when one pours 2 unit-volumes of liquid to 5 unit-volumes of liquid, one obtains 7 unit-volumes of liquid; rather, this is an application of the proposition which is appropriate only if no alteration of volume occurs, possibly as the result of a chemical reaction. Mill always confuses the application which one can make of an arithmetical proposition and which are often physical and do presuppose observed facts, with the purely mathematical proposition itself. To be sure, the plus-sign, in any of its applications, may appear to correspond to the process of making a heap, but that is not its meaning; for, given a different application, as for example when one relates calculations to events, there can be no question of heaps, aggregates or the relationship of a physical body to its parts. To be sure, here, too, one can speak of parts; but then one is not using the word in a physical or geometrical but a logical sense, as when one calls the murder of heads of states a part of murder as such. We here have a logical subordination. And so, too, addition generally does not correspond to physical states of affairs. Consequently the general laws of addition cannot be laws of nature either. . . .

Presumably the method of induction, if one understands by it not merely a habit, can itself be justified only by means of general propositions of arithmetic. As for a habit, it has no power whatever of generating truth. Whereas the method of

[11] Op. cit., Bk. II, chap. VI, § 3.

proceeding scientifically according to objective criteria now finds a high probability established in a single confirmation, now considers a thousandfold agreement worthless, a habit is determined by the number and strength of impressions and by subjective circumstances, which have no right whatever of exercising an influence on a judgment. Induction must base itself on the theory of probability, since it can never make a proposition more than probable. But how this theory could be developed without presupposing arithmetical laws is incomprehensible.

Bertrand Russell
(1872–1970)

What Is an
Empirical Science?

82 *Of the views so far presented, Russell's view comes closest
to that of Hobbes. Both agree that there are only two kinds of
truth, one of which is contingent or factual. They also agree that
all other truths (including mathematical truths) can be classed
together in a single group. Hobbes held that all non-factual
truths were such that if the subject term applied, we could
think of no case where the predicate term would not also
apply. It is easy to see how this holds for such truths as* **all
bachelors are unmarried** *and* **no grandmother is childless**
*which are "true by definition." It is less easy to see how truths
of mathematics can be shown to be of the same sort, as we
have seen from reading Frege.*

*Russell, on the other hand, felt that all non-empirical truths
were true in virtue of their form and independently sought to
establish that mathematical truths were ultimately formal
truths. But he also felt that such truths as* **all bachelors are
unmarried** *were really true in virtue of their form and that this
could be seen once one substituted synonymous expressions
for one another (i.e., substituted "unmarried male adult" for
"bachelor"). But it is one thing to say that a proposition is
true in virtue of its form and something else to say that it is
equivalent in meaning to some other proposition which is true
in virtue of its form. There also immediately arises for Russell,
as one who wishes to treat propositions which are true by
definition as being true by form, the question of what it is for
two expressions to be synonymous or equivalent in meaning.
As we shall see, this is the problem to which Quine addresses
himself in "Two Dogmas of Empiricism."*

From Bertrand Russell, *The Analysis of Matter*, Chapter VIII, pp. 170–
176. London: George Allen and Unwin Ltd., 1927. Copyright © 1927 by
George Allen and Unwin Ltd., 1954 by Dover Publications, Inc. Reprinted
by permission of the publishers.

It would be generally agreed that physics is an empirical science, as contrasted with logic and pure mathematics. I want, in this chapter, to define in what this difference consists.

We may observe, in the first place, that many philosophers in the past have denied the distinction. Thorough-going rationalists have believed that the facts which we regard as only discoverable by observation could really be deduced from logical and metaphysical principles; thorough-going empiricists have believed that the premisses of pure mathematics are obtained by induction from experience. Both views seem to me false, and are, I think, rarely held in the present day; nevertheless, it will be as well to examine the reasons for thinking that there is an epistemological distinction between pure mathematics and physics, before trying to discover its exact nature.

There is a traditional distinction between necessary and contingent propositions, and another between analytic and synthetic propositions. It was generally held before Kant that necessary propositions were the same as analytic propositions, and contingent propositions were the same as synthetic propositions. But even before Kant the two distinctions were different, even if they effected the same division of propositions. It was held that every proposition is necessary, assertoric, or possible, and that these are ultimate notions, comprised under the head of "modality." I do not think much can be made of modality, the plausibility of which seems to have come from confusing propositions with propositional functions. Propositions may, it is true, be divided in a way corresponding to what was meant by analytic and synthetic; this will be explained in a moment. But propositions which are not analytic can only be true or false; a true synthetic proposition cannot have a further property of being necessary, and a false synthetic proposition cannot have the property of being possible. Propositional functions, on the contrary, are of three kinds: those which are true for all values of the argument or arguments, those which are false for all values, and those which are true for some arguments and false for others. The first may be called necessary, the second impossible, the third possible. And these terms may be transferred to propositions when they are not known to be true on their own account, but what is known as to their truth or falsehood is deduced from knowledge of propositional functions. *E.g.* "it is possible that the next man I meet will be called John Smith" is a deduction from the fact that the propositional function "*x* is a man and is called John Smith" is possible—*i.e.* true for some values of *x* and false for others. Where, as in this instance, it is worth while to say that a *proposition* is possible, the fact rests upon our ignorance. With more knowledge, we should know who is the next man I shall meet, and then it would be certain that he is John Smith or certain that he is not John Smith. Possibility in this sense thus becomes assimilated to probability, and may count as any degree of probability other than 0 and 1. An "assertoric" proposition, similarly, was, I think, a confused notion applicable to a proposition known to be true but also known to be a value of a propositional function which is sometimes false—*e.g.* "John Smith is bald."

The distinction of analytic and synthetic is much more relevant to the difference between pure mathematics and physics. Traditionally, an "analytic" proposition was one whose contradictory was self-contradictory, or, what came to the same thing in Aristotelian logic, one which ascribed to a subject a predicate which was part of it—*e.g.* "white horses are horses." In practice, however, an analytic proposition was one whose truth could be known by means of logic alone. This meaning survives, and is still important, although we can no longer use the definition in terms of subject and predicate or that in terms of the law of contradiction. When Kant argued that "$7+5=12$" is synthetic, he was using the subject-predicate definition, as his argument shows. But when we define an analytic proposition as one which can be deduced from logic alone, then "$7+5=12$" is analytic. On the other hand, the proposition that the sum of the angles of a triangle is two right angles is synthetic. We must ask ourselves, therefore: What is the common quality of the propositions which can be deduced from the premisses of logic?

The answer to this question given by Wittgenstein in his *Tractatus Logico-Philosophicus* seems to me the right one. Propositions which form part of logic, or can be proved by logic, are all *tautologies*—*i.e.* they show that certain different sets of symbols are different ways of saying the same thing, or that one set says part of what the other says. Suppose I say: "If *p* implies *q*, then not-*q* implies not-*p*." Wittgenstein asserts that "*p* implies *q*" and "not-*q* implies not-*p*" are merely different symbols for one proposition: the fact which makes one true (or false) is the same as the fact which makes the other true (or false). Such propositions, therefore, are really concerned with symbols. We can know their truth or falsehood without studying the outside world, because they are only concerned with symbolic manipulations. I should add—

though here Wittgenstein might dissent—that all pure mathematics consists of tautologies in the above sense. If this is true, then obviously empiricists such as J. S. Mill are wrong when they say that we believe 2+2=4 because we have found so many instances of its truth that we can make an induction by simple enumeration which has little chance of being wrong. Every unprejudiced person must agree that such a view *feels* wrong: our certainty concerning simple mathematical propositions does not seem analogous to our certainty that the sun will rise to-morrow. I do not mean that we feel more sure of the one than of the other, though perhaps we ought to do so; I mean that our assurance seems to have a different source.

I accept the view, therefore, that some propositions are tautologies and some are not, and I regard this as the distinction underlying the old distinction of analytic and synthetic propositions. It is obvious that a proposition which is a tautology is so in virtue of its form, and that any constants which it may contain can be turned into variables without impairing its tautological quality. We may take as a stock example: "If Socrates is a man and all men are mortal, then Socrates is mortal." This is a value of the general logical tautology:

"For all values of x, a, and β, if x is an a, and all a's are β's, then x is a β."

In logic, it is a waste of time to deal with particular examples of general tautologies; therefore constants ought never to occur, except such as are purely formal. The cardinal numbers turn out to be purely formal in this sense; therefore all the constants of pure mathematics are purely formal.

A proposition cannot be a tautology unless it is of a certain complexity, exceeding that of the simplest propositions. It is obvious that there is more complexity in equating two ways of saying the same thing than there is in either way separately. It is obvious also that, whenever it is actually useful to know that two sets of symbols say the same thing, or that one says part of what the other says, that must be because we have some knowledge as to the truth or falsehood of what is expressed by one of the sets. Consequently logical knowledge would be very unimportant if it stood alone; its importance arises through its combination with knowledge of propositions which are not purely logical.

All the propositions which are not tautologies we shall call "synthetic." The simplest kinds of propositions must be synthetic, in virtue of the above argument. And if logic or pure mathematics can ever be employed in a process leading to knowledge that is not tautological, there must be sources of knowledge other than logic and pure mathematics.

The distinctions hitherto considered in this chapter have been logical. In the case of modality, it is true, we found a certain confusion from an admixture of epistemological notions; but modality was intended to be logical, and in one form it was found to be so. We come now to a distinction which is essentially epistemological, that, namely, between *a priori* and empirical knowledge.

Knowledge is said to be *a priori* when it can be acquired without requiring any fact of experience as a premiss; in the contrary case, it is said to be empirical. A few words are necessary to make the distinction clear. There is a process by which we acquire knowledge of dated events at times closely contiguous to them; this is the process called "perception" or "introspection"[1] according to the character of the events concerned. There is no doubt need of much discussion as to the nature of this process, and of still more as to the nature of the knowledge to be derived from it; but there can be no doubt of the broad fact that we do acquire knowledge in this way. We wake up and find that it is daylight, or that it is still night; we hear a clock strike; we see a shooting star; we read the newspaper; and so on. In all these cases we acquire knowledge of events, and the time at which we acquire the knowledge is the same, or nearly the same, as that at which the events take place. I shall call this process "perception," and shall, for convenience, include introspection—if this is really different from what is commonly called "perception." A fact of "experience" is one which we could not have known without the help of perception. But this is not quite clear until we have defined what we mean by "could not"; for clearly we may learn from experience that $2+2=4$, though we afterwards realize that the experience was not logically indispensable. In such cases, we see afterwards that the experience did not prove the proposition, but merely suggested it, and led to our finding the real proof. But, in view of the fact that the distinction between empirical and *a priori* is epistemological, not logical, it is obviously possible for a proposition to change from the one class to the other, since the classification in-

---

[1] I do not wish to prejudice the question whether there is such a process as "introspection," but only to include it *if* it exists.

volves reference to the organization of a particular person's knowledge at a particular time. So regarded, the distinction might seem unimportant; but it suggests some less subjective distinctions, which are what we really wish to consider.

Kant's philosophy started from the question: How are synthetic *a priori* judgments possible? Now we must first of all make a distinction. Kant is concerned with *knowledge,* not with mere *belief.* There is no philosophical problem in the fact that a man can have a *belief* which is synthetic and not based on experience—*e.g.* that this time the horse on which he has put his money will win. The philosophical problem arises only if there is a class of synthetic *a priori* beliefs which is always true. Kant considered the propositions of pure mathematics to be of this kind; but in this he was misled by the common opinion of his time, to the effect that geometry, though a branch of pure mathematics, gave information about actual space. Owing to non-Euclidean geometry, particularly as applied in the theory of relativity, we must now distinguish sharply between the geometry applicable to actual space, which is an empirical study forming part of physics, and the geometry of pure mathematics, which gives no information as to actual space. Consequently this instance of synthetic *a priori* knowledge, upon which Kant relied, is no longer available. Other kinds have been supposed to exist—for example, ethical knowledge, and the law of causality; but it is not necessary for our purposes to decide whether these kinds really exist or not. So far as physics is concerned, we may assume that all real knowledge is either dependent (at least in part) upon perception, or analytic in the sense in which pure mathematics is analytic. The Kantian synthetic *a priori* knowledge, whether it exists or not, seems not to be found in physics —unless, indeed, the principle of induction were to count as such.

But the principle of induction, as we have already seen, has its origin in physiology, and this suggests a quite different treatment of *a priori* beliefs from that of Kant. Whether there is *a priori knowledge* or not, there undoubtedly are, in a certain sense, *a priori beliefs.* We have reflexes which we intellectualize into beliefs; we blink, and this leads us to the belief that an object touching the eye will hurt it. We may have this belief before we have experience of its truth; if so, it is, in a sense, synthetic *a priori* knowledge—*i.e.* it is a belief, not based upon experience, in a true synthetic proposition. Our belief in induction is essentially analogous. But such beliefs, even when true, hardly deserve to be called knowledge, since they are not all true, and therefore all require verification before they ought to be regarded as certain. These beliefs have been useful in generating science, since they supplied hypotheses which were largely true; but they need not survive untested in modern science.

I shall therefore assume that, at any rate in every department relevant to physics, all knowledge is either analytic in the sense in which logic and pure mathematics are analytic, or is, at least in part, derived from perception. And all knowledge which is in any degree necessarily dependent upon perception I shall call "empirical." I shall regard a piece of knowledge as necessarily dependent upon perception when, after a careful analysis of our grounds for believing it, it is found that among these grounds there is the cognition of an event in time, arising at the same time as the event or very shortly after it, and fulfilling certain further criteria which are necessary in order to distinguish perception from certain kinds of error. These criteria will occupy us in the next chapter.

In a science, there are two kinds of empirical propositions. There are those concerned with particular matters of fact, and those concerned with laws induced from matters of fact. The appearances presented by the sun and moon and planets on certain occasions when they have been seen are particular matters of fact. The inference that the sun and moon and planets exist even when no one is observing them—in particular, that the sun exists at night and the planets by day—is an empirical induction. Heraclitus thought the sun was new every day, and there was no logical impossibility in this hypothesis. Thus empirical laws not only depend upon particular matters of fact, but are inferred from these by a process which falls short of logical demonstration. They differ from propositions of pure mathematics both through the nature of their premisses and through the method by which they are inferred from these premisses. . . .

Willard Van Orman Quine
(1908–   )

Two Dogmas of Empiricism

In this piece Quine argues that the analytic-synthetic distinc-   **89**
tion cannot be clearly made out and should be abandoned.
According to Quine, to try and set out the distinction in any
of the ways that this has been done historically is in the end
to suppose that we are able to substitute synonyms for each
other, thus reducing analytic truths to logical truths. But this
in turn presupposes that we have criteria for whether two expressions are synonymous. Such criteria, Quine argues, we do
not and cannot have.

Modern empiricism has been conditioned in large part by two
dogmas. One is a belief in some fundamental cleavage between
truths which are *analytic,* or grounded in meanings independently of matters of fact, and truths which are *synthetic,* or
grounded in fact. The other dogma is *reductionism:* the belief
that each meaningful *statement* is equivalent to some logical
construct upon terms which refer to immediate experience.
Both dogmas, I shall argue, are ill-founded. One effect of
abandoning them is, as we shall see, a blurring of the supposed boundary between speculative metaphysics and natural
science. Another effect is a shift toward pragmatism.

1. Background for Analyticity

Kant's cleavage between analytic and synthetic truths was
foreshadowed in Hume's distinction between relations of ideas

From Willard Van Orman Quine, *From a Logical Point of View,* Chapter
II, Parts 1–4, pp. 20–37. Cambridge: Harvard University Press, 1953. Copyright © 1953 by The President and Fellows of Harvard College. Reprinted
by permission of Harvard University Press, *The Philosophical Review,* and
the author.

and matters of fact, and in Leibniz's distinction between truths of reason and truths of fact. Leibniz spoke of the truths of reason as true in all possible worlds. Picturesqueness aside, this is to say that the truths of reason are those which could not possibly be false. In the same vein we hear analytic statements defined as statements whose denials are self-contradictory. But this definition has small explanatory value; for the notion of self-contradictoriness, in the quite broad sense needed for this definition of analyticity, stands in exactly the same need of clarification as does the notion of analyticity itself. The two notions are the two sides of a single dubious coin.

Kant conceived of an analytic statement as one that attributes to its subject no more than is already conceptually contained in the subject. This formulation has two shortcomings: it limits itself to statements of subject-predicate form, and it appeals to a notion of containment which is left at a metaphorical level. But Kant's intent, evident more from the use he makes of the notion of analyticity than from his definition of it, can be restated thus: a statement is analytic when it is true by virtue of meanings and independently of fact. Pursuing this line, let us examine the concept of *meaning* which is presupposed.

Meaning, let us remember, is not to be identified with naming. Frege's example of 'Evening Star' and 'Morning Star', and Russell's of 'Scott' and 'the author of *Waverley*', illustrate that terms can name the same thing but differ in meaning. The distinction between meaning and naming is no less important at the level of abstract terms. The terms '9' and 'the number of the planets' name one and the same abstract entity but presumably must be regarded as unlike in meaning; for astronomical observation was needed, and not mere reflection on meanings, to determine the sameness of the entity in question.

The above examples consist of singular terms, concrete and abstract. With general terms, or predicates, the situation is somewhat different but parallel. Whereas a singular term purports to name an entity, abstract or concrete, a general term does not; but a general term is *true of* an entity, or of each of many, or of none. The class of all entities of which a general term is true is called the *extension* of the term. Now paralleling the contrast between the meaning of a singular term and the entity named, we must distinguish equally between the meaning of a general term and its extension. The general terms 'creature with a heart' and 'creature with kidneys', for example, are perhaps alike in extension but unlike in meaning.

Confusion of meaning with extension, in the case of general terms, is less common than confusion of meaning with naming in the case of singular terms. It is indeed a commonplace in philosophy to oppose intension (or meaning) to extension, or, in a variant vocabulary, connotation to denotation.

The Aristotelian notion of essence was the forerunner, no doubt, of the modern notion of intension or meaning. For Aristotle it was essential in men to be rational, accidental to be two-legged. But there is an important difference between this attitude and the doctrine of meaning. From the latter point of view it may indeed be conceded (if only for the sake of argument) that rationality is involved in the meaning of the word 'man' while two-leggedness is not; but two-leggedness may at the same time be viewed as involved in the meaning of 'biped' while rationality is not. Thus from the point of view of the doctrine of meaning it makes no sense to say of the actual individual, who is at once a man and a biped, that his rationality is essential and his two-leggedness accidental or vice versa. Things had essences, for Aristotle, but only linguistic forms have meanings. Meaning is what essence becomes when it is divorced from the object of reference and wedded to the word.

For the theory of meaning a conspicuous question is the nature of its objects: what sort of things are meanings? A felt need for meant entities may derive from an earlier failure to appreciate that meaning and reference are distinct. Once the theory of meaning is sharply separated from the theory of reference, it is a short step to recognizing as the primary business of the theory of meaning simply the synonymy of linguistic forms and the analyticity of statements; meanings themselves, as obscure intermediary entities, may well be abandoned.

The problem of analyticity then confronts us anew. Statements which are analytic by general philosophical acclaim are not, indeed, far to seek. They fall into two classes. Those of the first class, which may be called *logically true,* are typified by:

1. No unmarried man is married.

The relevant feature of this example is that it not merely is true as it stands, but remains true under any and all reinterpretations of 'man' and 'married'. If we suppose a prior inventory of *logical* particles, comprising 'no', 'un-', 'not', 'if', 'then', 'and', etc., then in general a logical truth is a statement which is true and remains true under all reinterpretations of its components other than the logical particles.

But there is also a second class of analytic statements, typified by:

2. No bachelor is married.

The characteristic of such a statement is that it can be turned into a logical truth by putting synonyms for synonyms; thus (2) can be turned into (1) by putting 'unmarried man' for its synonym 'bachelor'. We still lack a proper characterization of this second class of analytic statements, and therewith of analyticity generally, inasmuch as we have had in the above description to lean on a notion of "synonymy" which is no less in need of clarification than analyticity itself.

In recent years Carnap has tended to explain analyticity by appeal to what he calls state-descriptions. A state-description is any exhaustive assignment of truth values to the atomic, or noncompound, statements of the language. All other statements of the language are, Carnap assumes, built up of their component clauses by means of the familiar logical devices, in such a way that the truth value of any complex statement is fixed for each state-description by specifiable logical laws. A statement is then explained as analytic when it comes out true under every state description. This account is an adaptation of Leibniz's "true in all possible worlds." But note that this version of analyticity serves its purpose only if the atomic statements of the language are, unlike 'John is a bachelor' and 'John is married', mutually independent. Otherwise there would be a state-description which assigned truth to 'John is a bachelor' and to 'John is married', and consequently 'No bachelors are married' would turn out synthetic rather than analytic under the proposed criterion. Thus the criterion of analyticity in terms of state-descriptions serves only for languages devoid of extra-logical synonym-pairs, such as 'bachelor' and 'unmarried man' —synonym-pairs of the type which give rise to the "second class" of analytic statements. The criterion in terms of state-descriptions is a reconstruction at best of logical truth, not of analyticity.

I do not mean to suggest that Carnap is under any illusions on this point. His simplified model language with its state-descriptions is aimed primarily not at the general problem of analyticity but at another purpose, the clarification of probability and induction. Our problem, however, is analyticity; and here the major difficulty lies not in the first class of analytic statements, the logical truths, but rather in the second class, which depends on the notion of synonymy.

2. Definition

There are those who find it soothing to say that the analytic statements of the second class reduce to those of the first class, the logical truths, by *definition;* 'bachelor', for example, is *defined* as 'unmarried man'. But how do we find that 'bachelor' is defined as 'unmarried man'? Who defined it thus, and when? Are we to appeal to the nearest dictionary, and accept the lexicographer's formulation as law? Clearly this would be to put the cart before the horse. The lexicographer is an empirical scientist, whose business is the recording of antecedent facts; and if he glosses 'bachelor' as 'unmarried man' it is because of his belief that there is a relation of synonymy between those forms, implicit in general or preferred usage prior to his own work. The notion of synonymy presupposed here has still to be clarified, presumably in terms relating to linguistic behavior. Certainly the "definition" which is the lexicographer's report of an observed synonymy cannot be taken as the ground of the synonymy.

Definition is not, indeed, an activity exclusively of philologists. Philosophers and scientists frequently have occasion to "define" a recondite term by paraphrasing it into terms of a more familiar vocabulary. But ordinarily such a definition, like the philologist's, is pure lexicography, affirming a relation of synonymy antecedent to the exposition in hand.

Just what it means to affirm synonymy, just what the interconnections may be which are necessary and sufficient in order that two linguistic forms be properly describable as synonymous, is far from clear; but, whatever these interconnections may be, ordinarily they are grounded in usage. Definitions reporting selected instances of synonymy come then as reports upon usage.

There is also, however, a variant type of definitional activity which does not limit itself to the reporting of preëxisting synonymies. I have in mind what Carnap calls *explication*—an activity to which philosophers are given, and scientists also in their more philosophical moments. In explication the purpose is not merely to paraphrase the definiendum into an outright synonym, but actually to improve upon the definiendum by refining or supplementing its meaning. But even explication, though not merely reporting a preëxisting synonymy between definiendum and definiens, does rest nevertheless on *other* preexisting synonymies. The matter may be viewed as follows. Any word worth explicating has some contexts which, as wholes, are clear and precise enough to be useful; and the purpose of explication is to preserve the usage of these favored contexts while sharpening the usage of other contexts. In order that a given definition be suitable for purposes of explication, therefore, what is required is not that the definiendum in its antecedent usage be synonymous with the definiens, but just that each of these favored contexts of the definiendum, taken as a whole in its antecedent usage, be synonymous with the corresponding context of the definiens.

Two alternative definientia may be equally appropriate for the purposes of a given task of explication and yet not be synonymous with each other; for they may serve interchangeably within the favored contexts but diverge elsewhere. By cleaving to one of these definientia rather than the other, a definition of explicative kind generates, by fiat, a relation of synonymy between definiendum and definiens which did not hold before. But such a definition still owes its explicative function, as seen, to preexisting synonymies.

There does, however, remain still an extreme sort of definition which does not hark back to prior synonymies at all: namely, the explicitly conventional introduction of novel notations for purposes of sheer abbreviation. Here the definiendum becomes synonymous with the definiens simply because it has been created expressly for the purpose of being synonymous with the definiens. Here we have a really transparent case of synonymy created by definition; would that all species of synonymy were as intelligible. For the rest, definition rests on synonymy rather than explaining it.

The word 'definition' has come to have a dangerously reassuring sound, owing no doubt to its frequent occurrence in logical and mathematical writings. We shall do well to digress now into a brief appraisal of the role of definition in formal work.

In logical and mathematical systems either of two mutually antagonistic types of economy may be striven for, and each has its peculiar practical utility. On the one hand we may seek economy of practical expression—ease and brevity in the statement of multifarious relations. This sort of economy calls usually for distinctive concise notations for a wealth of concepts. Second, however, and oppositely, we may seek economy in grammar and vocabulary; we may try to find a minimum of basic concepts such that, once a distinctive notation has been appropriated to each of them, it becomes possible to express any desired further concept by mere combination and iteration of our basic notations. This second sort of economy is impractical in one way, since a poverty in basic idioms tends to a necessary lengthening of discourse. But it is practical in another way: it greatly simplifies theoretical discourse *about* the language, through minimizing the terms and the forms of construction wherein the language consists.

Both sorts of economy, though prima facie incompatible, are valuable in their separate ways. The custom has consequently arisen of combining both sorts of economy by forging in effect two languages, the one a part of the other. The inclusive language, though redundant in grammar and vocabulary, is economical in message lengths, while the part, called primitive notation, is economical in grammar and vocabulary. Whole and part are correlated by rules of translation whereby each idiom not in primitive notation is equated to some complex built up of primitive notation. These rules of translation are the so-called *definitions* which appear in formalized systems. They are best viewed not as adjuncts to one language but as correlations between two languages, the one a part of the other.

But these correlations are not arbitrary. They are supposed to show how the primitive notations can accomplish all purposes, save brevity and convenience, of the redundant language. Hence the definiendum and its definiens may be expected, in each case, to be related in one or another of the three ways lately noted. The definiens may be a faithful paraphrase of the definiendum into the narrower notation, preserving a direct synonymy[1] as of antecedent usage; or the definiens may, in the spirit of explication, improve upon the antecedent usage of the definiendum; or finally, the definiendum may be a newly created notation, newly endowed with meaning here and now.

In formal and informal work alike, thus, we find that definition—except in the extreme case of the explicitly conventional introduction of new notations—hinges on prior relations of synonymy. Recognizing then that the notion of definition does not hold the key to synonymy and analyticity, let us look further into synonymy and say no more of definition.

---

[1] According to an important variant sense of 'definition', the relation preserved may be the weaker relation of mere agreement in reference. But definition in this sense is better ignored in the present connection, being irrelevant to the question of synonymy.

A natural suggestion, deserving close examination, is that the synonymy of two linguistic forms consists simply in their interchangeability in all contexts without change of truth value— interchangeability, in Leibniz's phrase, *salva veritate*. Note that synonyms so conceived need not even be free from vagueness, as long as the vaguenesses match.

But it is not quite true that the synonyms 'bachelor' and 'unmarried man' are everywhere interchangeable *salva veritate*. Truths which become false under substitution of 'unmarried man' for 'bachelor' are easily constructed with the help of 'bachelor of arts' or 'bachelor's buttons'; also with the help of quotation, thus:

'Bachelor' has less than ten letters.

Such counterinstances can, however, perhaps be set aside by treating the phrases 'bachelor of arts' and 'bachelor's buttons' and the quotation "bachelor" each as a single indivisible word and then stipulating that the interchangeability *salva veritate* which is to be the touchstone of synonymy is not supposed to apply to fragmentary occurrences inside of a word. This account of synonymy, supposing it acceptable on other counts, has indeed the drawback of appealing to a prior conception of "word" which can be counted on to present difficulties of formulation in its turn. Nevertheless some progress might be claimed in having reduced the problem of synonymy to a problem of wordhood. Let us pursue this line a bit, taking "word" for granted.

The question remains whether interchangeability *salva veritate* (apart from occurrences within words) is a strong enough condition for synonymy, or whether, on the contrary, some heteronymous expressions might be thus interchangeable. Now let us be clear that we are not concerned here with synonymy in the sense of complete identity in psychological associations or poetic quality; indeed no two expressions are synonymous in such a sense. We are concerned only with what may be called *cognitive* synonymy. Just what this is cannot be said without successfully finishing the present study; but we know something about it from the need which arose for it in connection with analyticity in §1. The sort of synonymy needed there was merely such that any analytic statement could be turned into a logical truth by putting synonyms for synonyms. Turning the tables and assuming analyticity, indeed, we could explain cognitive synonymy of terms as follows (keeping to the familiar example): to say that 'bachelor' and 'unmarried man' are cognitively synonymous is to say no more nor less than that the statement:

3. All and only bachelors are unmarried men

is analytic.[2]

What we need is an account of cognitive synonymy not presupposing analyticity—if we are to explain analyticity conversely with help of cognitive synonymy as undertaken in §1. And indeed such an independent account of cognitive synonymy is at present up for consideration, namely, interchangeability *salva veritate* everywhere except within words. The question before us, to resume the thread at last, is whether such interchangeability is a sufficient condition for cognitive synonymy. We can quickly assure ourselves that it is, by examples of the following sort. The statement:

4. Necessarily all and only bachelors are bachelors

is evidently true, even supposing 'necessarily' so narrowly construed as to be truly applicable only to analytic statements. Then, if 'bachelor' and 'unmarried man' are interchangeable *salva veritate,* the result:

5. Necessarily all and only bachelors are unmarried men

of putting 'unmarried man' for an occurrence of 'bachelor' in (4) must, like (4), be true. But to say that (5) is true is to say that (3) is analytic, and hence that 'bachelor' and 'unmarried man' are cognitively synonymous.

Let us see what there is about the above argument that gives it its air of hocus-pocus. The condition of interchangeability *salva veritate* varies in its force with variations in the richness of the language at hand. The above argument supposes we are working with a language rich enough to contain the adverb 'necessarily', this adverb being so construed as to yield truth when and only when applied to an analytic statement. But can we condone a language which contains such an adverb? Does the adverb really make sense? To suppose that it does is to

---

[2] This is cognitive synonymy in a primary, broad sense. Carnap and Lewis have suggested how, once this notion is at hand, a narrower sense of cognitive synonymy which is preferable for some purposes can in turn be derived. But this special ramification of concept-building lies aside from the present purposes and must not be confused with the broad sort of cognitive synonymy here concerned.

suppose that we have already made satisfactory sense of 'analytic'. Then what are we so hard at work on right now?

Our argument is not flatly circular, but something like it. It has the form, figuratively speaking, of a closed curve in space.

Interchangeability *salva veritate* is meaningless until relativized to a language whose extent is specified in relevant respects. Suppose now we consider a language containing just the following materials. There is an indefinitely large stock of one-place predicates (for example, *'F'* where *'Fx'* means that x is a man) and many-place predicates (for example, *'G'* where *'Gxy'* means that x loves y), mostly having to do with extralogical subject matter. The rest of the language is logical. The atomic sentences consist each of a predicate followed by one or more variables *'x', 'y'*, etc.; and the complex sentences are built up of the atomic ones by truth functions ('not', 'and', 'or', etc.) and quantification. In effect such a language enjoys the benefits also of descriptions and indeed singular terms generally, these being contextually definable in known ways. Even abstract singular terms naming classes, classes of classes, etc., are contextually definable in case the assumed stock of predicates includes the two-place predicate of class membership. Such a language can be adequate to classical mathematics and indeed to scientific discourse generally, except in so far as the latter involves debatable devices such as contrary-to-fact conditionals or modal adverbs like 'necessarily'. Now a language of this type is extensional, in this sense: any two predicates which agree extensionally (that is, are true of the same objects) are interchangeable *salva veritate.*

In an extensional language, therefore, interchangeability *salva veritate* is no assurance of cognitive synonymy of the desired type. That 'bachelor' and 'unmarried man' are interchangeable *salva veritate* in an extensional language assures us of no more than that (3) is true. There is no assurance here that the extensional agreement of 'bachelor' and 'unmarried man' rests on meaning rather than merely on accidental matters of fact, as does the extensional agreement of 'creature with a heart' and 'creature with kidneys'.

For most purposes extensional agreement is the nearest approximation to synonymy we need care about. But the fact remains that extensional agreement falls far short of cognitive synonymy of the type required for explaining analyticity in the manner of §1. The type of cognitive synonymy required there is such as to equate the synonymy of 'bachelor' and 'unmarried man' with the analyticity of (3), not merely with the truth of (3).

So we must recognize that interchangeability *salva veritate,* if construed in relation to an extensional language, is not a sufficient condition of cognitive synonymy in the sense needed for deriving analyticity in the manner of §1. If a language contains an intensional adverb 'necessarily' in the sense lately noted, or other particles to the same effect, then interchangeability *salva veritate* in such a language does afford a sufficient condition of cognitive synonymy; but such a language is intelligible only in so far as the notion of analyticity is already understood in advance.

The effort to explain cognitive synonymy first, for the sake of deriving analyticity from it afterward as in §1, is perhaps the wrong approach. Instead we might try explaining analyticity somehow without appeal to cognitive synonymy. Afterward we could doubtless derive cognitive synonymy from analyticity satisfactorily enough if desired. We have seen that cognitive synonymy of 'bachelor' and 'unmarried man' can be explained as analyticity of (3). The same explanation works for any pair of one-place predicates, of course, and it can be extended in obvious fashion to many-place predicates. Other syntactical categories can also be accommodated in fairly parallel fashion. Singular terms may be said to be cognitively synonymous when the statement of identity formed by putting '=' between them is analytic. Statements may be said simply to be cognitively synonymous when their biconditional (the result of joining them by 'if and only if') is analytic.[3] If we care to lump all categories into a single formulation, at the expense of assuming again the notion of "word" which was appealed to early in this section, we can describe any two linguistic forms as cognitively synonymous when the two forms are interchangeable (apart from occurrences within "words") *salva* (no longer *veritate* but) *analyticitate.* Certain technical questions arise, indeed, over cases of ambiguity or homonymy; let us not pause for them, however, for we are already digressing. Let us rather turn our backs on the problem of synonymy and address ourselves anew to that of analyticity.

4. Semantical Rules

Analyticity at first seemed most naturally definable by appeal to a realm of meanings. On refinement, the appeal to meanings gave way to an appeal to synonymy or definition. But

---

[3] The 'if and only if' itself is intended in the truth functional sense.

definition turned out to be a will-o'-the-wisp, and synonymy turned out to be best understood only by dint of a prior appeal to analyticity itself. So we are back at the problem of analyticity.

I do not know whether the statement 'Everything green is extended' is analytic. Now does my indecision over this example really betray an incomplete understanding, an incomplete grasp of the 'meanings', of 'green' and 'extended'? I think not. The trouble is not with 'green' or 'extended', but with 'analytic'.

It is often hinted that the difficulty in separating analytic statements from synthetic ones in ordinary language is due to the vagueness of ordinary language and that the distinction is clear when we have a precise artificial language with explicit 'semantical rules.' This, however, as I shall now attempt to show, is a confusion.

The notion of analyticity about which we are worrying is a purported relation between statements and languages: a statement S is said to be *analytic for* a language $L,$ and the problem is to make sense of this relation generally, that is, for variable 'S' and 'L'. The gravity of this problem is not perceptibly less for artificial languages than for natural ones. The problem of making sense of the idiom 'S is analytic for L', with variable 'S' and 'L', retains its stubbornness even if we limit the range of the variable 'L' to artificial languages. Let me now try to make this point evident.

For artificial languages and semantical rules we look naturally to the writings of Carnap. His semantical rules take various forms, and to make my point I shall have to distinguish certain of the forms. Let us suppose, to begin with, an artificial language L_0 whose semantical rules have the form explicitly of a specification, by recursion or otherwise, of all the analytic statements of L_0. The rules tell us that such and such statements, and only those, are the analytic statements of L_0. Now here the difficulty is simply that the rules contain the word 'analytic', which we do not understand! We understand what expressions the rules attribute analyticity to, but we do not understand what the rules attribute to those expressions. In short, before we can understand a rule which begins 'A statement S is analytic for language L_0 if and only if . . .', we must understand the general relative term 'analytic for'; we must understand 'S is analytic for L' where 'S' and 'L' are variables.

Alternatively we may, indeed, view the so-called rule as a conventional definition of a new simple symbol 'analytic-for-L_0', which might better be written untendentiously as 'K' so as not to seem to throw light on the interesting word 'analytic'.

Obviously any number of classes K, M, N, etc. of statements of L_0 can be specified for various purposes or for no purpose; what does it mean to say that K, as against M, N, etc., is the class of the "analytic" statements of L_0?

By saying what statements are analytic for L_0 we explain 'analytic-for-L_0' but not 'analytic', nor 'analytic for'. We do not begin to explain the idiom 'S is analytic for L' with variable 'S' and 'L', even if we are content to limit the range of 'L' to the realm of artificial languages.

Actually we do know enough about the intended significance of 'analytic' to know that analytic statements are supposed to be true. Let us then turn to a second form of semantical rule, which says not that such and such statements are analytic but simply that such and such statements are included among the truths. Such a rule is not subject to the criticism of containing the un-understood word 'analytic'; and we may grant for the sake of argument that there is no difficulty over the broader term 'true'. A semantical rule of this second type, a rule of truth, is not supposed to specify all the truths of the language; it merely stipulates, recursively or otherwise, a certain multitude of statements which, along with others unspecified, are to count as true. Such a rule may be conceded to be quite clear. Derivatively, afterward, analyticity can be demarcated thus: a statement is analytic if it is (not merely true but) true according to the semantical rule.

Still there is really no progress. Instead of appealing to an unexplained word 'analytic', we are now appealing to an unexplained phrase 'semantical rule'. Not every true statement which says that the statements of some class are true can count as a semantical rule—otherwise *all* truths would be "analytic" in the sense of being true according to semantical rules. Semantical rules are distinguishable, apparently, only by the fact of appearing on a page under the heading 'Semantical Rules'; and this heading is itself then meaningless.

We can say indeed that a statement is *analytic-for-L_0* if and only if it is true according to such and such specifically appended "semantical rules," but then we find ourselves back at essentially the same case which was originally discussed: 'S is analytic-for-L_0 if and only if. . . .' Once we seek to explain 'S is analytic for L' generally for variable 'L' (even allowing limitation of 'L' to artificial languages), the explanation 'true according to the semantical rules of L' is unavailing; for the relative term 'semantical rule of' is as much in need of clarification, at least, as 'analytic for'.

It may be instructive to compare the notion of semantical rule with that of postulate. Relative to a given set of postulates, it is easy to say what a postulate is: it is a member of the set. Relative to a given set of semantical rules, it is equally easy to say what a semantical rule is. But given simply a notation, mathematical or otherwise, and indeed as thoroughly understood a notation as you please in point of the translations or truth conditions of its statements, who can say which of its true statements rank as postulates? Obviously the question is meaningless—as meaningless as asking which points in Ohio are starting points. Any finite (or effectively specifiable infinite) selection of statements (preferably true ones, perhaps) is as much a set of postulates as any other. The word 'postulate' is significant only relative to an act of inquiry; we apply the word to a set of statements just in so far as we happen, for the year or the moment, to be thinking of those statements in relation to the statements which can be reached from them by some set of transformations to which we have seen fit to direct our attention. Now the notion of semantical rule is as sensible and meaningful as that of postulate, if conceived in a similarly relative spirit—relative, this time, to one or another particular enterprise of schooling unconversant persons in sufficient conditions for truth of statements of some natural or artificial language L. But from this point of view no one signalization of a subclass of the truths of L is intrinsically more a semantical rule than another; and, if 'analytic' means 'true by semantical rules', no one truth of L is analytic to the exclusion of another.

It might conceivably be protested that an artificial language L (unlike a natural one) is a language in the ordinary sense *plus* a set of explicit semantical rules—the whole constituting, let us say, an ordered pair; and that the semantical rules of L then are specifiable simply as the second component of the pair L. But, by the same token and more simply, we might construe an artificial language L outright as an ordered pair whose second component is the class of its analytic statements; and then the analytic statements of L become specifiable simply as the statements in the second component of L. Or better still, we might just stop tugging at our bootstraps altogether.

Not all the explanations of analyticity known to Carnap and his readers have been covered explicitly in the above considerations, but the extension to other forms is not hard to see. Just one additional factor should be mentioned which sometimes enters: sometimes the semantical rules are in effect rules of translation into ordinary language, in which case the analytic statements of the artificial language are in effect recognized as such from the analyticity of their specified translations in ordinary language. Here certainly there can be no thought of an illumination of the problem of analyticity from the side of the artificial language.

From the point of view of the problem of analyticity the notion of an artificial language with semantical rules is a *feu follet par excellence.* Semantical rules determining the analytic statements of an artificial language are of interest only in so far as we already understand the notion of analyticity; they are of no help in gaining this understanding.

Appeal to hypothetical languages of an artificially simple kind could conceivably be useful in clarifying analyticity, if the mental or behavioral or cultural factors relevant to analyticity—whatever they may be—were somehow sketched into the simplified model. But a model which takes analyticity merely as an irreducible character is unlikely to throw light on the problem of explicating analyticity.

It is obvious that truth in general depends on both language and extralinguistic fact. The statement 'Brutus killed Caesar' would be false if the world had been different in certain ways, but it would also be false if the word 'killed' happened rather to have the sense of 'begat'. Thus one is tempted to suppose in general that the truth of a statement is somehow analyzable into a linguistic component and a factual component. Given this supposition, it next seems reasonable that in some statements the factual component should be null; and these are the analytic statements. But, for all its a priori reasonableness, a boundary between analytic and synthetic statements simply has not been drawn. That there is such a distinction to be drawn at all is an unempirical dogma of empiricists, a metaphysical article of faith.

John Austin
(1911–1960)

The Meaning of a Word

104   *Austin calls attention to cases where there exists something like a contradiction but where the traditional characterizations of analyticity do not seem to apply.* **It is raining, but I do not believe it** *seems at least analogous to a self-contradictory assertion. But* **if it is raining, then I believe it** *is not, by any standard criteria, analytic. Austin goes on to challenge what he calls the "working model" of language which goes hand in hand with the analytic-synthetic distinction.*

. . . Constantly we ask the question, 'Is *y* the meaning, or *part* of the meaning, or *contained* in the meaning, of *x*?—or is it *not*?' A favourite way of putting the question is to ask, 'Is the judgement "*x* is *y*" analytic or synthetic?' Clearly, we suppose, *y must* be *either* a part of the meaning of *x, or* not any part of it. And, if *y is* a part of the meaning of *x,* to say '*x* is not *y*' will be self-contradictory: while if it is *not* a part of the meaning of *x,* to say '*x* is not *y*' will present no difficulty—such a state of affairs will be readily 'conceivable'. This seems to be the merest common sense. And no doubt it *would* be the merest common sense *if* 'meanings' were things in some ordinary sense which contained parts in some ordinary sense. But they are *not.* Unfortunately, many philosophers who know they are not, still speak as though *y* must either be or not be 'part of the meaning' of *x.* But this is the point: *if* 'explaining the meaning of a word' is really the complicated sort of affair that we have seen it to be, and *if* there is really nothing to call 'the meaning of a word'—*then* phrases like 'part of the meaning of the word *x*' are completely undefined; it is left hanging in the

From J. L. Austin, *Philosophical Papers,* Section II, pp. 30–37. Oxford: Oxford University Press, 1961. Copyright © 1961 by Oxford University Press. Reprinted by permission of the Clarendon Press, Oxford.

air, we do not know what it means at all. *We are using a working-model which fails to fit the facts that we really wish to talk about.* When we consider what we really do want to talk about, and not the working-model, what would really be meant at all by a judgement being 'analytic or synthetic'? We simply do not know. Of course, we feel inclined to say 'I can easily produce examples of analytic and synthetic judgements; for instance, I should confidently say "Being a professor is *not* part of the meaning of being a man" and so forth'. 'A is A is analytic'. Yes, but it is when we are required to give a *general definition* of what we mean by 'analytic' or 'synthetic', and when we are required to justify our dogma that *every* judgement is either analytic or synthetic, that we find we have, in fact, nothing to fall back upon *except our working-model.* From the start, it is clear that our working-model fails to do justice, for example, to the distinction between syntactics and semantics: for instance, talking about the contradictory of every sentence having to be either self-contradictory or not so, is to talk as though all sentences which we are prohibited from saying were sentences which offended against *syntactical* rules, and could be formally reduced to verbal self-contradictions. But this overlooks all semantical considerations, which philosophers are sadly prone to do. Let us consider two cases of some things which we simply *cannot say:* although they are *not* 'self-contradictory' and although—and this of course is where many will have axes to grind—we cannot possibly be tempted to say that we have 'synthetic *a priori*' knowledge of their contradictions.

Let us begin with a case which, being about *sentences* rather than *words,* is not quite in point, but which may encourage us. Take the well-known sentence 'The cat is on the mat, and I do not believe it'. That seems absurd. On the other hand 'The cat is on the mat, and I believe it' seems trivial. If we were to adopt a customary dichotomy, and to say *either* a proposition *p* implies another proposition *r, or p* is perfectly compatible with not-*r,* we should at once in our present case be tempted to say that 'The cat is on the mat' *implies* 'I believe it': hence both the triviality of adding 'and I believe it' and the absurdity of adding 'and I do not believe it'. But of course 'the cat is on the mat' does *not* imply 'Austin believes the cat is on the mat': nor even 'the speaker believes the cat is on the mat'—for the speaker may be lying. The doctrine which is produced in this case is, that not *p* indeed, but *asserting p* implies 'I (who assert *p*) believe *p*'. And here 'implies' must be given a special sense: for of course it is not 'I assert *p'* implies (in the ordinary sense) 'I believe *p*', for I may be lying. It is the sort of sense in which by asking a question I 'imply' that I do not know the answer to it. By asserting *p* I *give it to be understood* that I believe *p.*

Now the reason why I cannot say 'The cat is on the mat and I do not believe it' is not that it offends against syntactics in the sense of being in some way 'self-contradictory'. What prevents my saying it, is rather some semantic convention (implicit, of course), about the way we use words *in situations.* What precisely is the account to be given in this case we need not ask. Let us rather notice one significant feature of it. Whereas '*p* and I believe it' is somehow trivial, and '*p* and I do not believe it' is somehow nonsense, a third sentence '*p* and *I might not have* believed it' makes perfectly good sense. Let us call these three sentences Q, not Q, and 'might not Q'. Now what prohibits us from saying '*p*' implies 'I believe *p*' in the ordinary sense of 'implies', is precisely shown by this fact: that although not-Q is (*somehow*) absurd, 'might not Q' is not at all absurd. For in ordinary cases of implication, not merely is not Q absurd, but 'might not Q' is *also* absurd: e.g., 'triangles are figures and triangles have no shape' is no more absurd than 'triangles are figures and triangles might have had no shape'. Consideration of the sentence 'might not Q' will afford a rough test as to whether *p* 'implies' *r* in the *ordinary* sense, or in the special sense, of 'implies'.

Bearing this in mind, let us now consider a sentence which, as I claim, cannot possibly be classified as *either* 'analytic' *or* 'synthetic'. I refer to the sentence, 'This *x* exists', where *x* is a sensum, e.g. 'This noise exists'. In endeavouring to classify it, one party would point to the triviality of 'This noise exists', and to the absurdity of 'This noise does not exist'. They would say, therefore, that *existence* is 'part of the meaning of' *this.* But another party would point out, that 'This noise might not have existed' makes perfectly good sense. *They* would say, therefore, that *existence* cannot be 'part of the meaning of' *this.*

Both parties, as we are now in a position to see, would be correct in their *arguments,* but incorrect in their *conclusions.* What seems to be true is that *using the word 'this'* (not: the word 'this') *gives it to be understood that* the sensum referred to 'exists'.

Perhaps, historically, this fact about the sentence-trio, 'This noise exists', 'This noise does not exist', and 'This noise might not have existed', was pointed out before any philosopher had had time to pronounce that 'This noise exists' is analytic, or is synthetic. But such a pronouncement might well have been made: and *to this day,* even when the fact has been pointed out, many philosophers *worry* about the case, supposing the sentence *must* be one or the other but painfully aware of the difficulties in choosing either. I wish to point out that consideration of the analogy between this case and the other, should cure us once and for all of this bogy, and of insisting on classifying sentences as *either* analytic *or* synthetic. It may encourage us to consider again what the facts in their actual complexity really are. (One thing it suggests is a reconsideration of 'Caesar is bald' and similar propositions: but I cannot go into that.)

So far, however, we have scarcely begun in earnest: we have merely felt that initial trepidation, experienced when the firm ground of prejudice begins to slip away beneath the feet. Perhaps there are other cases, or other sorts of cases, where it will not be possible to say either that *y* is a 'part of the meaning' of *x* or that it is not, without being misleading.

Suppose we take the case of 'being thought good by me' and 'being approved of by me'. Are we to rush at this with the dichotomy: *either* 'being approved of by me' *is* part of the meaning of 'being thought good by me' *or* it is *not*? Is it *obvious* that 'I think *x* good but I do not approve of it' is self-contradictory? Of course It is not *verbally* self-contradictory. That it either is or is not 'really' self-contradictory would seem to be difficult to establish. Of course, we think, it must be one or the other—only 'it's difficult to decide *which*': or 'it depends on how you use the words'. But are those really the difficulties which baffle us? Of course, *if* it were certain that every sentence *must* be either analytic or synthetic, those *must* be the difficulties. But then, it is not certain: no account even of what the distinction means, is given except by reference to our shabby working-model. I suggest that 'I think *x* good but I do not approve of it' may very well be neither self-contradictory nor yet 'perfectly good sense' in the way in which 'I think *x* exciting but I do not approve of it' *is* 'perfectly good sense'.

Perhaps this example does not strike you as awkward. It cannot be expected that all examples will appeal equally to all hearers. Let us take some others. Is 'What is good ought to exist' analytic or synthetic? According to Moore's theory, this must be 'synthetic': yet he constantly in *Principia Ethica* takes its truth for granted. And that illustrates one of the main drawbacks of insisting on saying that a sentence *must* be either analytic or synthetic: you are almost certain to have left on your hands some general sentences which are certainly not analytic but which you find it difficult to conceive being false: i.e. you are landed with 'synthetic *a priori* knowledge'. Take that sentence of ill fame 'Pink is more like red than black'. It is rash to pronounce this 'synthetic *a priori* knowledge' on the ground that 'being more like red than black' is not 'part of the meaning' or 'part of the definition' of 'pink' and that it is not 'conceivable' that pink should be more like black than red: I dare say, so far as those phrases have any clear meaning, that it *is not*: but the question is: *is* the thing therefore 'synthetic' *a priori* knowledge?

Or, again, take some examples from Berkeley: is *extended* 'part of the meaning' of *coloured* or of *shaped,* or *shaped* 'part of the meaning' of *extended*? Is 'est sed non percipitur' self-contradictory (when said of a sensum), or is it not? When we worry thus, is it not worth considering the possibility that we are oversimplifying?

What we are to say in these cases, what even the possibilities are, I do not at present clearly see. (1) Evidently, we must throw away the old working-model as soon as we take account even of the existence of a distinction between syntactics and semantics. (2) But evidently also, our *new* working-model, the supposed 'ideal' language, is in many ways a most inadequate model of any *actual* language: its careful separation of syntactics from semantics, its lists of explicitly formulated rules and conventions, and its careful delimitation of their spheres of operation—all are misleading. An *actual* language has few, if any, explicit conventions, no sharp limits to the spheres of operation of rules, no rigid separation of what is syntactical and what semantical. (3) Finally, I think I can see that there are difficulties about our powers of imagination, and about the curious way in which it is enslaved by words.

To encourage ourselves in the belief that this sort of consideration may play havoc with the distinction 'analytic or synthetic', let us consider a similar and more familiar case. It seems, does it not, perfectly obvious that every proposition must have a contradictory? Yet it does not turn out so. Suppose that I live in harmony and friendship for four years with a cat: and then it delivers a philippic. We ask ourselves, perhaps, 'Is it a real cat? or is it *not* a real cat?' 'Either it *is,* or it *is not,* but we cannot be sure which.' Now actually, that is not so: *neither* 'It is a real cat' *nor* 'it is not a real cat' fits the facts semantically: each is designed for other situations than this one: you could not say the former of something which delivers philippics, nor yet the latter of something which has behaved as this has for four years. There are similar difficulties about choosing between 'This *is* a hallucination' and 'This is *not* a hallucination'. With sound instinct, the plain man turns in such cases to Watson and says 'Well now, *what would you say*?' 'How would you *describe* it?' The difficulty is just that: there is *no* short description which is not misleading: the only thing to do, and that can easily be done, is to set out the description of the facts at length. Ordinary language breaks down in extraordinary cases. (In such cases, the cause of the breakdown is semantical.) Now no doubt an *ideal* language would *not* break down, whatever happened. In doing physics, for example, where our language is tightened up in order precisely to describe complicated and unusual cases concisely, we *prepare linguistically for the worst.* In ordinary language we do not: *words fail us.* If we talk as though an ordinary must be like an ideal language, we shall misrepresent the facts.

Consider now 'being extended' and 'being shaped'. In ordinary life we never get into a situation where we learn to say that anything is extended but not shaped nor conversely. We have all learned to use, and have used, the words only in cases where it is correct to use both. Supposing now someone says '*x* is extended but has no shape'. Somehow we cannot see what this 'could mean'—there are no semantic conventions, explicit or implicit, to cover this case: yet it is not prohibited in any way—there are no limiting rules about what we might or might not say *in extraordinary cases.* It is not *merely* the difficulty of imagining or experiencing extraordinary cases, either, which causes worry. There is this too: we can only describe what it is we are trying to imagine, by means of words which precisely describe and evoke the *ordinary* case, which we are trying to think away. Ordinary language *blinkers* the already feeble imagination. It would be difficult, in this way, if I were to say 'Can I think of a case where a man would be neither at home nor not at home?' This is inhibiting, because I think of the *ordinary* case where I ask 'Is he at home?' and get the answer, 'No': when certainly he is not at home. But supposing I happen *first* to think of the situation when I call on him just after he has died: then I see at once it would be wrong to say either. So in our case, the only thing to do is to imagine or experience all kinds of odd situations, and then suddenly round on oneself and ask: there, *now* would I say that, being extended, it must be shaped? A new idiom might in odd cases be demanded.

I should like to say, in concluding this section, that in the course of stressing that we must pay attention to the facts of *actual* language, what we can and cannot say, and *precisely* why, another and converse point takes shape. Although it will not do to force actual language to accord with some preconceived model: it *equally* will not do, having discovered the facts about 'ordinary usage' *to rest content* with that, as though there were nothing more to be discussed and discovered. There may be plenty that might happen and does happen which would need new and better language to describe it in. Very often philosophers are only engaged on this task, when they seem to be perversely using words in a way which makes no sense according to 'ordinary usage'. There may be extraordinary facts, even about our everyday experience, which plain men and plain language overlook.

H. P. Grice
(1913–   )
P. F. Strawson
(1919–   )

In Defense of a
Dogma

In this piece Grice and Strawson work to salvage the analytic-synthetic distinction from Quine's attack. For the most part they disagree not with the considerations Quine offers about meaning and language but rather with what these considerations can be taken to show about the analytic-synthetic distinction.

The last several pages of the Grice-Strawson piece examine sections of Quine's article (section 5 and 6) which were not included in this volume. Since the relevant passages are given by Grice and Strawson, however, this should cause the reader no difficulty.

However successful Grice and Strawson may be in defending the coherence and usefulness of the analytic-synthetic distinction, it is clear that new issues have been raised by this controversy, and one in particular promises to be very rich. This is the question of what criteria one shall use to judge whether a given concept, as expressed in a language, has over a period of time undergone change so that we can say that a different concept has emerged, or that a term now has a new or different sense. Few philosophers would claim that this question will be quickly or easily answered.

111

In his article "Two Dogmas of Empiricism," Professor Quine advances a number of criticisms of the supposed distinction

From H. P. Grice and P. F. Strawson, "In Defense of a Dogma," *Philosophical Review*, LXV, 2, April 1956, pp. 141–158. Reprinted by permission of the *Philosophical Review* and the authors.

between analytic and synthetic statements, and of other associated notions. It is, he says, a distinction which he rejects. We wish to show that his criticisms of the distinction do not justify his rejection of it.

There are many ways in which a distinction can be criticized, and more than one in which it can be rejected. It can be criticized for not being a sharp distinction (for admitting of cases which do not fall clearly on either side of it); or on the ground that the terms in which it is customarily drawn are ambiguous (have more than one meaning); or on the ground that it is confused (the different meanings being habitually conflated). Such criticisms alone would scarcely amount to a rejection of the distinction. They would, rather, be a prelude to clarification. It is not this sort of criticism which Quine makes.

Again, a distinction can be criticized on the ground that it is not useful. It can be said to be useless for certain purposes, or useless altogether, and, perhaps, pedantic. One who criticizes in this way may indeed be said to reject a distinction, but in a sense which also requires him to acknowledge its existence. He simply declares he can get on without it. But Quine's rejection of the analytic-synthetic distinction appears to be more radical than this. He would certainly say he could get on without the distinction, but not in a sense which would commit him to acknowledging its existence.

Or again, one could criticize the way or ways in which a distinction is customarily expounded or explained on the ground that these explanations did not make it really clear. And Quine certainly makes such criticisms in the case of the analytic-synthetic distinction.

But he does, or seems to do, a great deal more. He declares, or seems to declare, not merely that the distinction is useless or inadequately clarified, but also that it is altogether illusory, that the belief in its existence is a philosophical mistake. "That there is such a distinction to be drawn at all," he says, "is an unempirical dogma of empiricists, a metaphysical article of faith." It is the existence of the distinction that he here calls in question; so his rejection of it would seem to amount to a denial of its existence.

Evidently such a position of extreme skepticism about a distinction is not in general justified merely by criticisms, however just in themselves, of philosophical attempts to clarify it. There are doubtless plenty of distinctions, drawn in philosophy and outside it, which still await adequate philosophical elucidation, but which few would want on this account to declare illusory. Quine's article, however, does not consist wholly, though it does consist largely, in criticizing attempts at eluci- dation. He does try also to diagnose the causes of the belief in the distinction, and he offers some positive doctrine, ac- ceptance of which he represents as incompatible with this belief. If there is any general prior presumption in favor of the existence of the distinction, it seems that Quine's radical re- jection of it must rest quite heavily on this part of his article, since the force of any such presumption is not even impaired by philosophical failures to clarify a distinction so supported.

Is there such a presumption in favor of the distinction's existence? Prima facie, it must be admitted that there is. An appeal to philosophical tradition is perhaps unimpressive and is certainly unnecessary. But it is worth pointing out that Quine's objection is not simply to the words "analytic" and "synthetic," but to a distinction which they are supposed to express, and which at different times philosophers have sup- posed themselves to be expressing by means of such pairs of words or phrases as "necessary" and "contingent," "a priori" and "empirical," "truth of reason" and "truth of fact"; so Quine is certainly at odds with a philosophical tradition which is long and not wholly disreputable. But there is no need to appeal only to tradition; for there is also present practice. We can appeal, that is, to the fact that those who use the terms "analytic" and "synthetic" do to a very considerable extent agree in the applications they make of them. They apply the term "analytic" to more or less the same cases, withhold it from more or less the same cases, and hesitate over more or less the same cases. This agreement extends not only to cases which they have been *taught* so to characterize, but to new cases. In short, "analytic" and "synthetic" have a more or less established philosophical *use;* and this seems to suggest that it is absurd, even senseless, to say that there is no such dis- tinction. For, in general, if a pair of contrasting expressions are habitually and generally used in application to the same cases, *where these cases do not form a closed list,* this is a sufficient condition for saying that there are *kinds* of cases to which the expressions apply; and nothing more is needed for them to mark a distinction.

In view of the possibility of this kind of argument, one may begin to doubt whether Quine really holds the extreme thesis which his words encourage one to attribute to him. It is for this reason that we made the attribution tentative. For on at least one natural interpretation of this extreme thesis, when we say of something true that it is analytic and of another true thing that it is synthetic, it simply never is the case that we thereby mark a distinction between them. And this view seems terribly difficult to reconcile with the fact of an established philosophical usage (i.e., of general agreement in application in an open class). For this reason, Quine's thesis might be better represented not as the thesis that there is *no difference at all* marked by the use of these expressions, but as the thesis that the nature of, and reasons for, the difference or differences are totally misunderstood by those who use the expressions, that the stories they tell themselves *about* the difference are full of illusion.

We think Quine might be prepared to accept this amendment. If so, it could, in the following way, be made the basis of something like an answer to the argument which prompted it. Philosophers are notoriously subject to illusion, and to mistaken theories. Suppose there were a particular mistaken theory about language or knowledge, such that, seen in the light of this theory, some statements (or propositions or sentences) appeared to have a characteristic which no statements really have, or even, perhaps, which it does not make sense to suppose that any statement has, and which no one who was not consciously or subconsciously influenced by this theory would ascribe to any statement. And suppose that there were other statements which, seen in this light, did not appear to have this characteristic, and others again which presented an uncertain appearance. Then philosophers who were under the influence of this theory would tend to mark the supposed presence or absence of this characteristic by a pair of contrasting expressions, say "analytic" and "synthetic." Now in these circumstances it still could not be said that there was no distinction at all being marked by the use of these expressions, for there would be at least the distinction we have just described (the distinction, namely, between those statements which appeared to have and those which appeared to lack a certain characteristic), and there might well be other assignable differences too, which would account for the difference in appearance; but it certainly could be said that *the* difference these philosophers supposed themselves to be marking by the use of the expressions simply did not exist, and perhaps also (supposing the characteristic in question to be one which it was absurd to ascribe to any statement) that these expressions, as so used, were senseless or without meaning. We should only have to suppose that such a mistaken theory was very plausible and attractive, in order to reconcile the fact of an established philosophical usage for a pair of contrasting terms with the claim that *the* distinction which the terms purported to mark did not exist at all, though not with the claim that there simply did not exist a difference of any kind between the classes of statements so characterized. We think that the former claim would probably be sufficient for Quine's purposes. But to establish such a claim on the sort of grounds we have indicated evidently requires a great deal more argument than is involved in showing that certain explanations of a term do not measure up to certain requirements of adequacy in philosophical clarification—and not only more argument, but argument of a very different kind. For it would surely be too harsh to maintain that the *general* presumption is that philosophical distinctions embody the kind of illusion we have described. On the whole, it seems that philosophers are prone to make too few distinctions rather than too many. It is their assimilations, rather than their distinctions, which tend to be spurious.

So far we have argued as if the prior presumption in favor of the existence of the distinction which Quine questions rested solely on the fact of an agreed *philosophical* usage for the terms "analytic" and "synthetic." A presumption with only this basis could no doubt be countered by a strategy such as we have just outlined. But, in fact, if we are to accept Quine's account of the matter, the presumption in question is not only so based. For among the notions which belong to the analyticity-group is one which Quine calls "cognitive synonymy," and in terms of which he allows that the notion of analyticity could at any rate be formally explained. Unfortunately, he adds, the notion of cognitive synonymy is just as unclarified as that of analyticity. To say that two expressions *x* and *y* are cognitively synonymous seems to correspond, at any rate roughly, to what we should ordinarily express by saying that *x* and *y* have the same meaning or that *x* means the same as *y*. If Quine is to be consistent in his adherence to the extreme thesis, then it appears that he must maintain not only that the distinction we suppose ourselves to be marking by the use of the terms "analytic" and "synthetic" does not exist, but also that the distinction we suppose ourselves to be marking by the use of the expressions "means the same as," "does not mean the same as" does not exist either. At least, he must maintain this insofar as the notion of *meaning the same as,* in its application to predicate-expressions, is supposed to differ from and

go beyond the notion of *being true of just the same objects as.*
(This latter notion—which we might call that of "coextensionality"—he is prepared to allow to be intelligible, though, as he
rightly says, it is not sufficient for the explanation of analyticity.) Now since he cannot claim this time that the pair of
expressions in question (viz., "means the same," "does not
mean the same") is the special property of philosophers, the
strategy outlined above of countering the presumption in favor
of their marking a genuine distinction is not available here
(or is at least enormously less plausible). Yet the denial that
the distinction (taken as different from the distinction between
the coextensional and the non-coextensional) really exists, is
extremely paradoxical. It involves saying, for example, that
anyone who seriously remarks that "bachelor" means the
same as "unmarried man" but that "creature with kidneys"
does not mean the same as "creature with a heart"—supposing the last two expressions to be coextensional—*either* is not
in fact drawing attention to any distinction at all between the
relations between the members of each pair of expressions *or*
is making a philosophical mistake about the nature of the distinction between them. In either case, what he says, taken as
he intends it to be taken, is senseless or absurd. More generally, it involves saying that it is always senseless or absurd
to make a statement of the form "Predicates *x* and *y* in fact
apply to the same objects, but do not have the same meaning."
But the paradox is more violent than this. For we frequently
talk of the presence or absence of relations of synonymy between kinds of expressions—e.g., conjunctions, particles of
many kinds, whole sentences—where there does not appear
to be any obvious substitute for the ordinary notion of synonymy, in the way in which coextensionality is said to be a
substitute for synonymy of predicates. Is all such talk meaningless? Is all talk of correct or incorrect *translation* of
sentences of one language into sentences of another meaningless? It is hard to believe that it is. But if we do successfully
make the effort to believe it, we have still harder renunciations
before us. If talk of sentence-synonymy is meaningless, then
it seems that talk of sentences having a meaning at all must
be meaningless too. For if it made sense to talk of a sentence
having a meaning, or meaning something, then presumably it
would make sense to ask "What does it mean?" And if it made
sense to ask "What does it mean?" of a sentence, then sentence-synonymy could be roughly defined as follows: Two
sentences are synonymous if and only if any true answer to

the question "What does it mean?" asked of one of them, is a true answer to the same question, asked of the other. We do not, of course, claim any clarifying power for this definition. We want only to point out that if we are to give up the notion of sentence-synonymy as senseless, we must give up the notion of sentence-significance (of a sentence having meaning) as senseless too. But then perhaps we might as well give up the notion of sense.—It seems clear that we have here a typical example of a philosopher's paradox. Instead of examining the actual use that we make of the notion of *meaning the same,* the philosopher measures it by some perhaps inappropriate standard (in this case some standard of clarifiability), and because it falls short of this standard, or seems to do so, denies its reality, declares it illusory.

We have argued so far that there is a strong presumption in favor of the existence of the distinction, or distinctions, which Quine challenges—a presumption resting both on philosophical and on ordinary usage—and that this presumption is not in the least shaken by the fact, if it is a fact, that the distinctions in question have not been, in some sense, adequately clarified. It is perhaps time to look at what Quine's notion of adequate clarification is.

The main theme of his article can be roughly summarized as follows. There is a certain circle or family of expressions, of which "analytic" is one, such that if any one member of the circle could be taken to be satisfactorily understood or explained, then other members of the circle could be verbally, and hence satisfactorily, explained in terms of it. Other members of the family are: "self-contradictory" (in a broad sense), "necessary," "synonymous," "semantical rule," and perhaps (but again in a broad sense) "definition." The list could be added to. Unfortunately each member of the family is in as great need of explanation as any other. We give some sample quotations: "The notion of self-contradictoriness (in the required broad sense of inconsistency) stands in exactly the same need of clarification as does the notion of analyticity itself." Again, Quine speaks of "a notion of synonymy which is in no less need of clarification than analyticity itself." Again, of the adverb "necessarily," as a candidate for use in the explanation of synonymy, he says, "Does the adverb *really make sense?* To suppose that it does is to suppose that we have already *made satisfactory sense* of 'analytic.' To make "satisfactory sense" of one of these expressions would seem to involve two things. (1) It would seem to involve providing an explanation which does not incorporate any expression belonging to the family-circle. (2) It would seem that the explanation provided must be of the same general character as those rejected explanations which do incorporate members of the family-circle (i.e., it must specify some feature common and peculiar to all cases to which, for example, the word "analytic" is to be applied; it must have the same general form as an explanation beginning, "a statement is analytic if and only if . . ."). It is true that Quine does not explicitly state the second requirement; but since he does not even consider the question whether any other kind of explanation would be relevant, it seems reasonable to attribute it to him. If we take these two conditions together, and generalize the result, it would seem that Quine requires of a satisfactory explanation of an expression that it should take the form of a pretty strict definition but should not make use of any member of a group of interdefinable terms to which the expression belongs. We may well begin to feel that a satisfactory explanation is hard to come by. The other element in Quine's position is one we have already commented on in general, before enquiring what (according to him) is to count as a satisfactory explanation. It is the step from "We have not made satisfactory sense (provided a satisfactory explanation) of *x*" to "*x* does not make sense."

It would seem fairly clearly unreasonable to insist *in general* that the availability of a satisfactory explanation in the sense sketched above is a necessary condition of an expression's making sense. It is perhaps dubious whether *any* such explanations can *ever* be given. (The hope that they can be is, or was, the hope of reductive analysis in general.) Even if such explanations can be given in some cases, it would be pretty generally agreed that there are other cases in which they cannot. One might think, for example, of the group of expressions which includes "morally wrong," "blameworthy," "breach of moral rules," etc.; or of the group which includes the propositional connectives and the words "true" and "false," "statement," "fact," "denial," "assertion." Few people would want to say that the expressions belonging to either of these groups were senseless on the ground that they have not been formally defined (or even on the ground that it was impossible formally to define them) except in terms of members of the same group. It might, however, be said that while the unavailability of a satisfactory explanation in the special sense described was not a *generally* sufficient reason for declaring that a given expression was senseless, it was a sufficient reason in the case of the expressions of the analyticity group. But anyone who said this would have to advance a reason for discriminating in this way against the expressions of this group. The only plausible reason for being harder on these expressions than on others is a refinement on a consideration which we have already had before us. It starts from the point that "analytic" and "synthetic" themselves are technical philosophical expressions. To the rejoinder that other expressions of the family concerned, such as "means the same as" or "is inconsistent with," or "self-contradictory," are not at all technical expressions, but are common property, the reply would doubtless be that, to qualify for inclusion in the family circle, these expressions have to be used in specially adjusted and precise senses (or pseudo-senses) which they do not ordinarily possess. It is the fact, then, that all the terms belonging to the circle are *either* technical terms *or* ordinary terms used in specially adjusted senses, that might be held to justify us in being particularly suspicious of the claims of members of the circle to have any sense at all, and hence to justify us in requiring them to pass a test for significance which would admittedly be too stringent if generally applied. This point has some force, though we doubt if the special adjustments spoken of are in every case as considerable as it suggests. (This seems particularly doubtful in the case of the word "inconsistent"—a perfectly good member of the nontechnician's meta-logical vocabulary.) But though the point has some force, it does not have whatever force would be required to justify us in insisting that the expressions concerned should pass exactly that test for significance which is in question. The fact, if it is a fact, that the expressions cannot be explained in precisely the way which Quine seems to require, does not mean that they cannot be explained at all. There is no need to try to pass them off as expressing innate ideas. They can be and are explained, though in other and less formal ways than that which Quine considers. (And the fact that they are so explained fits with the facts, first, that there is a generally agreed philosophical use for them, and second, that this use is technical or specially adjusted.) To illustrate the point briefly for one member of the analyticity family. Let us suppose we are trying to explain to someone the notion of *logical impossibility* (a member of the family which Quine presumably regards as no clearer than any of the others) and we decide to do it by bringing out the contrast between logical and natural (or causal) impossibility. We might take as our examples the logical impossibility of a child of three's being an adult, and the natural impossibility of a child of three's understanding Russell's Theory of Types. We might instruct our pupil to imagine two conversations one of which begins by someone (X) making the claim:

    1. "My neighbor's three-year-old child understands Russell's Theory of Types,"

and the other of which begins by someone (Y) making the claim:

    1′. "My neighbor's three-year-old child is an adult."

It would not be inappropriate to reply to X, taking the remarks as a hyperbole:

    2. "You mean the child is a particularly bright lad."

If X were to say:

    3. "No, I mean what I say—he really does understand it,"

one might be inclined to reply:

    4. "I don't believe you—the thing's impossible."

But if the child were then produced, and did (as one knows he would not) expound the theory correctly, answer questions on it, criticize it, and so on, one would in the end be forced to acknowledge that the claim was literally true and that the child was a prodigy. Now consider one's reaction to Y's claim. To begin with, it might be somewhat similar to the previous case. One might say:

    2′. "You mean he's uncommonly sensible or very advanced for his age."

If Y replies:

    3′. "No, I mean what I say,"

we might reply:

    4′. "Perhaps you mean that he won't grow any more, or that he's a sort of freak, that he's already fully developed."

Y replies:

    5′. "No, he's not a freak, he's just an adult."

At this stage—or possibly if we are patient, a little later—we shall be inclined to say that we just don't understand what Y is saying, and to suspect that he just does not know the meaning of some of the words he is using. For unless he is prepared to admit that he is using words in a figurative or unusual sense, we shall say, not that we don't believe him, but that his words have *no* sense. And whatever kind of creature is ultimately produced for our inspection, it will not lead us to say that what Y said was literally true, but at most to say that we now see what he meant. As a summary of the difference between the two imaginary conversations, we might say that in both cases we would tend to begin by supposing that the other speaker was using words in a figurative or unusual or restricted way; but in the face of his repeated claim to be speaking literally, it would be appropriate in the first case to say that we did not believe him and in the second case to say that we did not understand him. If, like Pascal, we thought it prudent to prepare against very long chances, we should in the first case know what to prepare for; in the second, we should have no idea.

We give this as an example of just one type of informal explanation which we might have recourse to in the case of one notion of the analyticity group. (We do not wish to suggest it is the only type.) Further examples, with different though connected types of treatment, might be necessary to teach our pupil the use of the notion of logical impossibility in its application to more complicated cases—if indeed he did not pick it up from the one case. Now of course this type of explanation does not yield a formal statement of necessary and sufficient conditions for the application of the notion concerned. So it does not fulfill one of the conditions which Quine seems to require of a satisfactory explanation. On the other hand, it does appear to fulfill the other. It breaks out of the family circle. The distinction in which we ultimately come to rest is that between not believing something and not understanding something; or between incredulity yielding to conviction, and incomprehension yielding to comprehension. It would be rash to maintain that *this* distinction does not need clarification; but it would be absurd to maintain that it does not exist. In the face of the availability of this informal type of explanation for the notions of the analyticity group, the fact that they have not received another type of explanation (which it is dubious whether *any* expressions *ever* receive) seems a wholly inadequate ground for the conclusion that the notions are pseudo-notions, that the expressions which purport to express them have no sense. To say this is not to deny that it would be philosophically desirable, and a proper object of philosophical endeavor, to find a more illuminating general characterization of the notions of this group than any that has been so far given. But the question of how, if at all, this can be done is quite irrelevant to the question of whether or not the expressions which belong to the circle have an intelligible use and mark genuine distinctions.

So far we have tried to show that sections 1 to 4 of Quine's article—the burden of which is that the notions of the analyticity group have not been satisfactorily explained—do not establish the extreme thesis for which he appears to be arguing. It remains to be seen whether sections 5 and 6, in which diagnosis and positive theory are offered, are any more successful. But before we turn to them, there are two further points worth making which arise out of the first two sections.

1. One concerns what Quine says about *definition* and *synonymy.* He remarks that definition does not, as some have supposed, "hold the key to synonymy and analyticity," since "definition—except in the extreme case of the explicitly conventional introduction of new notations—hinges on prior relations of synonymy." But now consider what he says of these extreme cases. He says: "Here the definiendum becomes synonymous with the definiens simply because it has been expressly created for the purpose of being synonymous with the definiens. Here we have a really transparent case of synonymy created by definition; would that all species of synonymy were as intelligible." Now if we are to take these words of Quine seriously, then his position *as a whole* is incoherent. It is like the position of a man to whom we are trying to explain, say, the idea of one thing fitting into another thing, or two things fitting together, and who says: "I can understand what it means to say that one thing fits into another, or that two things fit together, in the case where one was specially made to fit the other; but I cannot understand what it means to say this in any other case." Perhaps we should not take Quine's words here too seriously. But if not, then we have the right to ask him exactly what state of affairs he thinks *is* brought about by explicit definition, what relation between expressions *is* established by this procedure, and why he thinks it unintelligible to suggest that the same (or a closely analogous) state of affairs, or relation, should exist in the absence of this procedure. For our part, we should be inclined to take Quine's words (or some of them) seriously, and reverse his conclusions; and maintain that the notion of synonymy by explicit convention would be unintelligible if the notion of synonymy by usage were not presupposed. There cannot be law where there is no custom, or rules where there are not practices (though perhaps we can understand better what a practice is by looking at a rule).

2. The second point arises out of a paragraph on page 32 of Quine's book. We quote:

I do not know whether the statement "Everything green is extended" is analytic. Now does my indecision over this example really betray an incomplete understanding, an incomplete grasp, of the "meanings" of "green" and "extended"? I think not. The trouble is not with "green" or "extended," but with "analytic."

If, as Quine says, the trouble is with "analytic," then the trouble should doubtless disappear when "analytic" is removed. So let us remove it, and replace it with a word which Quine himself has contrasted favorably with "analytic" in respect of perspicuity—the word "true." Does the indecision at once disappear? We think not. The indecision over "analytic" (and equally, in this case, the indecision over "true") arises, of course, from a further indecision: viz., that which we feel when confronted with such questions as "Should we count a *point* of green light as *extended* or not?" As is frequent enough in such cases, the hesitation arises from the fact that the boundaries of application of words are not determined by usage in all possible directions. But the example Quine has chosen is particularly unfortunate for his thesis, in that it is only too evident that our hesitations are not *here* attributable to obscurities in "analytic." It would be possible to choose other examples in which we should hesitate between "analytic" and "synthetic" and have few qualms about 'true." But no more in these cases than in the sample case does the hesitation necessarily imply any obscurity in the notion of analyticity; since the hesitation would be sufficiently accounted for by the same or a similar kind of indeterminacy in the relations between the words occurring within the statement about which the question, whether it is analytic or synthetic, is raised.

Let us now consider briefly Quine's positive theory of the relations between the statements we accept as true or reject as false on the one hand and the "experiences" in the light of which we do this accepting and rejecting on the other. This theory is boldly sketched rather than precisely stated. We shall merely extract from it two assertions, one of which Quine clearly takes to be incompatible with acceptance of the distinction between analytic and synthetic statements, and the other of which he regards as barring one way to an explanation of that distinction. We shall seek to show that the first assertion is not incompatible with acceptance of the distinction, but is, on the contrary, most intelligibly interpreted in a way quite consistent with it, and that the second assertion leaves the way open to just the kind of explanation which Quine thinks it precludes. The two assertions are the following:

1. It is an illusion to suppose that there is any class of accepted statements the members of which are in principle "immune from revision" in the light of experience, i.e., any that we accept as true and must continue to accept as true whatever happens.

2. It is an illusion to suppose that an individual statement, taken in isolation from its fellows, can admit of confirmation or disconfirmation at all. There is no particular statement such that a particular experience or set of experiences decides once for all whether that statement is true or false, independently of our attitudes to all other statements.

The apparent connection between these two doctrines may be summed up as follows. Whatever our experience may be, it is in principle possible to hold on to, or reject, any particular statement we like, so long as we are prepared to make extensive enough revisions elsewhere in our system of beliefs. In practice our choices are governed largely by considerations of convenience: we wish our system to be as simple as possible, but we also wish disturbances to it, as it exists, to be as small as possible.

The apparent relevance of these doctrines to the analytic-synthetic distinction is obvious in the first case, less so in the second.

1. Since it is an illusion to suppose that the characteristic of immunity in principle from revision, come what may, belongs, or could belong, to any statement, it is an illusion to suppose that there is a distinction to be drawn between statements which possess this characteristic and statements which lack it. Yet, Quine suggests, this is precisely the distinction which those who use the terms "analytic" and "synthetic" suppose themselves to be drawing. Quine's view would perhaps also be (though he does not explicitly say this in the article under consideration) that those who believe in the distinction are inclined at least sometimes to mistake the characteristic of strongly resisting revision (which belongs to beliefs very centrally situated in the system) for the mythical characteristic of total immunity from revision.

2. The connection between the second doctrine and the analytic-synthetic distinction runs, according to Quine, through the verification theory of meaning. He says: "If the verification theory can be accepted as an adequate account of statement synonymy, the notion of analyticity is saved after all." For, in

the first place, two statements might be said to be synonymous if and only if any experiences which contribute to, or detract from, the confirmation of one contribute to, or detract from, the confirmation of the other, to the same degree; and, in the second place, synonymy could be used to explain analyticity. But, Quine seems to argue, acceptance of any such account of synonymy can only rest on the mistaken belief that individual statements, taken in isolation from their fellows, can admit of confirmation or disconfirmation at all. As soon as we give up the idea of a set of experiential truth-conditions for each statement taken separately, we must give up the idea of explaining synonymy in terms of identity of such sets.

Now to show that the relations between these doctrines and the analytic-synthetic distinction are not as Quine supposes. Let us take the second doctrine first. It is easy to see that acceptance of the second doctrine would not compel one to abandon, but only to revise, the suggested explanation of synonymy. Quine does not deny that individual statements are regarded as confirmed or disconfirmed, are in fact rejected or accepted, in the light of experience. He denies only that these relations between single statements and experience can confirm or disconfirm an individual statement, only given certain assumptions about the truth or falsity of other statements. When we are faced with a "recalcitrant experience," he says, we always have a choice of what statements to amend. What we have to renounce is determined by what we are anxious to keep. This view, however, requires only a slight modification of the definition of statement-synonymy in terms of confirmation and disconfirmation. All we have to say now is that two statements are synonymous if and only if any experiences which, *on certain assumptions about the truth-values of other statements,* confirm or disconfirm one of the pair, also, *on the same assumptions,* confirm or disconfirm the other to the same degree. More generally, Quine wishes to substitute for what he conceives to be an oversimple picture of the confirmation-relations between particular statements and particular experiences, the idea of a looser relation which he calls "germaneness" (p. 43). But however loosely "germaneness" is to be understood, it would apparently continue to make sense to speak of two statements as standing in the same germaneness-relation to the same particular experiences. So Quine's views are not only consistent with, but even suggest, an amended account of statement-synonymy along these lines. We are not, of course, concerned to defend such account, or even to state it with any precision. We are only concerned to show that acceptance of Quine's doctrine of empirical confirmation does not, as he says it does, entail giving up the attempt to define statement-synonymy in terms of confirmation.

Now for the doctrine that there is no statement which is in principle immune from revision, no statement which might not be given up in the face of experience. Acceptance of this doctrine is quite consistent with adherence to the distinction between analytic and synthetic statements. Only, the adherent of *this* distinction must also insist on another; on the distinction between that kind of giving up which consists in merely admitting falsity, and that kind of giving up which involves changing or dropping a concept or set of concepts. Any form of words at one time held to express something true may, no doubt, at another time, come to be held to express something false. But it is not only philosophers who would distinguish between the case where this happens as the result of a change of opinion solely as to matters of fact, and the case where this happens at least partly as a result of a shift in the sense of the words. Where such a shift in the sense of the words is a necessary condition of the change in truth-value, then the adherent of the distinction will say that the form of words in question changes from expressing an analytic statement to expressing a synthetic statement. We are not now concerned, or called upon, to elaborate an adequate theory of conceptual revision, any more than we were called upon, just now, to elaborate an adequate theory of synonymy. If we can make sense of the idea that the same form of words, taken in one way (or bearing one sense), may express something true, and taken in another way (or bearing another sense), may express something false, then we can make sense of the idea of conceptual revision. And if we can make sense of this idea, then we can perfectly well preserve the distinction between the analytic and the synthetic, while conceding to Quine the revisability-in-principle of everything we say. As for the idea that the same form of words, taken in different ways, may bear different senses and perhaps be used to say things with different truth-values, the onus of showing that this is somehow a mistaken or confused idea rests squarely on Quine. The point of substance (or one of them) that Quine is making, by this emphasis on revisability, is that there is no absolute necessity about the adoption or use of any conceptual scheme whatever, or, more narrowly and in terms that he would reject, that there is no analytic proposition such that we *must* have linguistic forms bearing just the sense required to express that proposition. But it is one thing to admit this, and quite another thing to say that there are no necessities within any conceptual scheme we adopt or use, or, more narrowly again, that there are no linguistic forms which do express analytic propositions.

The adherent of the analytic-synthetic distinction may go further and admit that there may be cases (particularly perhaps in the field of science) where it would be pointless to press the question whether a change in the attributed truth-value of a statement represented a conceptual revision or not, and correspondingly pointless to press the analytic-synthetic distinction. We cannot quote such cases, but this inability may well be the result of ignorance of the sciences. In any case, the existence, if they do exist, of statements about which it is pointless to press the question whether they are analytic or synthetic, does not entail the nonexistence of statements which are clearly classifiable in one or other of these ways and of statements our hesitation over which has different sources, such as the possibility of alternative interpretations of the linguistic forms in which they are expressed.

This concludes our examination of Quine's article. It will be evident that our purpose has been wholly negative. We have aimed to show merely that Quine's case against the existence of the analytic-synthetic distinction is not made out. His article has two parts. In one of them, the notions of the analyticity group are criticized on the ground that they have not been adequately explained. In the other, a positive theory of truth is outlined, purporting to be incompatible with views to which believers in the analytic-synthetic distinction either must be, or are likely to be, committed. In fact, we have contended, no single point is established which those who accept the notions of the analyticity group would feel any strain in accommodating in their own system of beliefs. This is not to deny that many of the points raised are of the first importance in connection with the problem of giving a satisfactory general account of analyticity and related concepts. We are here only criticizing the contention that these points justify the rejection, as illusory, of the analytic-synthetic distinction and the notions which belong to the same family.

Bibliography

Books

Aristotle. *The Works of Aristotle,* W. D. Ross, ed., Oxford, **129**
1908–1931:
    De Interpretatione, E. M. Edghill, trans, pp. 12 ff.
    Metaphysics, W. D. Ross, trans., V.5 and VI.2.
    Physics, R. P. Hardie and R. K. Gaye, trans., II.9.
    Posterior Analytics, G. R. G. Mure, trans., I.1 ff.,
    especially I.6.

Austin, John L. *Philosophical Papers,* "The Meaning of a Word"
(Chapter 2), Oxford: Clarendon, 1961, pp. 23–43. Section
2 reprinted in this volume.

Ayer, Alfred Jules. *Language, Truth and Logic,* Chapter 4, London: Gollancz, 1958 (first published 1936; revised 1946),
pp. 71–87. Reprinted in Paul Benacerraf and Hilary Putnam, eds., *Philosophy of Mathematics,* "The A Priori,"
Englewood Cliffs, N.J.: Prentice-Hall, 1964, pp. 289–301;
John V. Canfield and Franklin H. Donnell, eds., *Readings
in the Theory of Knowledge,* New York: Appleton-Century-
Crofts, 1964, pp. 237–249; Paul Edwards and Arthur Pap,
eds., *A Modern Introduction to Philosophy,* New York:
Free Press, 1957, pp. 646–657; Joel Feinberg, ed., *Reason
and Responsibility,* "The A Priori," Belmont, Calif.: Dickenson, 1965, pp. 161–169 and L. W. Sumner and John
Woods, eds., *Necessary Truth: A Book of Readings,* New
York: Random, 1969, pp. 27–43.

Bain, Alexander. *Logic, London:* Longmans, Green, 1910.

Bergmann, Gustav. *Logic and Reality,* Chapter 13, Madison,
Wisconsin: University of Wisconsin Press, 1964, pp. 272–
301.

Blanshard, Brand. *The Nature of Thought,* Vol. II, Chapter IV, New York: Macmillan, 1955 (first published 1939), pp. 335–520.

Bosanquet, Bernard. *Logic,* 2nd Ed. Vol. I, Chapter 1, Oxford: Clarendon, 1911. "Analytic and Synthetic," reprinted in Ernest Nagel and Richard B. Brandt, eds., *Systematic Readings in Epistemology,* New York: Harcourt, 1965, pp. 199–202.

Britton, Karl. *Communication,* Chapter 7, London: K. Paul, Trench, Trubner, 1939.

Bunge, Mario Augusto. *The Myth of Simplicity,* Chapter 2, Englewood Cliffs, N.J.: Prentice-Hall, 1963.

Carnap, Rudolf. *Logical Foundations of Probability,* Chapter 3, Chicago: University of Chicago Press, 1950.

———. *Meaning and Necessity,* Chapter 2, Chicago: University of Chicago Press, 1947.

Chisholm, Roderick M. *Theory of Knowledge,* Chapter 5, Englewood Cliffs, N.J.: Prentice-Hall, 1966.

Cohen, Laurence Jonathan. *The Diversity of Meaning,* Chapter 6, London: Methuen, 1962.

Crawshay-Williams, R. *Methods and Criteria of Reasoning,* Chapter 13, London: Routledge and Kegan Paul; New York: Humanities Press, 1957.

Ewing, Alfred Cyril. *The Fundamental Questions of Philosophy,* Chapter 2, New York: Macmillan, 1951.

———. *Idealism, A Critical Survey,* Chapter 4, London: Methuen, 1961.

Frege, Gottlob. *The Foundations of Arithmetic* (1884), especially Sections 1–17 and 87–91, Oxford: Blackwell, 1950. Sections 5–11 reprinted in this volume.

Harré, R., ed. *The Principles of Linguistic Philosophy,* by Friedrich Waismann, Chapter 3 ("Is There *A Priori* Knowledge?"), New York: St. Martin's, 1965, pp. 44–67.

Hobbes, Thomas. Sir William Molesworth, ed., *The English Works of Thomas Hobbes,* "Of Propositions," London: John Bohn, 1838, pp. 29–44. Pages 37–38 reprinted in this volume.

Hospers, John. *An Introduction to Philosophical Analysis,* Chapter 2, Englewood Cliffs, N.J.: Prentice-Hall, 1953.

Hume, David. L. A. Selby-Bigge, ed., *Treatise of Human Nature,* London: Oxford University Press (1888), 1967.

Joseph, Horace William Brindley. *An Introduction to Logic,* (2nd ed. 1916, pp. 207–215.) Reprinted, Oxford: Clarendon, 1957.

Kant, Immanuel. Norman Kemp Smith, trans., *Critique of Pure Reason* (1781), Introduction, Sections 1–4 and *passim,* New York: St. Martin's, 1961. Sections 1–6 ("How Are *A Priori* Synthetic Judgments Possible?") reprinted in John V. Canfield and Franklin H. Donnell, Jr., eds., *Readings in the Theory of Knowledge,* New York: Appleton-Century-Crofts, 1964, pp. 177–186; Paul Edwards and Arthur Pap, eds., *A Modern Introduction to Philosophy,* New York: Free Press, 1957, pp. 612–623; Sections 1–4 reprinted in L. W. Sumner and John Woods, eds., *Necessary Truth: A Book of Readings,* New York: Random, 1969, pp. 10–17; also reprinted in this volume.

———. *Prolegomena . . .* (1783), Peter G. Lucus, ed., Manchester: Manchester University Press, 1953, Sections 2–3.

Kneale, William, and Martha Kneale. *The Development of Logic,* Chapter 10, Section 5, Oxford: Clarendon, 1962.

Laird, John. *Knowledge, Belief, and Opinion,* Chapter 8, New York: The Century Co., 1930.

———. *A Study in Realism.* Chapter 6. Cambridge, England: The University Press, 1920.

Lazerowitz, Morris. *The Structure of Metaphysics,* Chapter 12. ("Logical Necessity"), London: Routledge and Kegan Paul, 1955, pp. 254–276.

Leibniz, Gottfried Wilhelm. L. E. Loemker, ed., *Philosophical Papers and Letters,* "On Freedom" and "First Truths," Dordrecht: D. Reidel, 1969. "First Truths" reprinted in this volume.

Lewis, Clarence Irving. *An Analysis of Knowledge and Valuation,* Chapters 5, 6, La Salle, Ill: Open Court, 1946.

———. *Mind and the World Order,* Chapters 7–9, New York: Dover, 1929 and 1956.

McCosh, James. *An Examination of Mr. J. S. Mill's Philosophy,* New York: R. Carter and Brothers, 1880.

Martin, Richard Milton. *The Notion of Analytic Truth,* Philadelphia: University of Pennsylvania Press, 1959.

Mill, John Stuart. *A System of Logic,* "Demonstration and Necessary Truths," London: Longmans, Green, 1879. pp. 258–299. Excerpts reprinted in this volume.

Mitchell, David. *An Introduction to Logic,* Chapter 8, London: Hutchinson University Library, 1962.

Nagel, Ernest. *Logic Without Metaphysics,* Chapters 3–5, Glencoe, Ill.: Free Press, 1956.

Pap, Arthur. *The A Priori in Physical Theory,* New York: Russell and Russell, 1968.

———. *Elements of Analytic Philosophy,* Chapters 6, 16b, c, New York: Macmillan, 1949.

———. *Semantics and Necessary Truth,* New Haven: Yale University Press, 1958. Sections reprinted in L. W. Sumner and John Woods, eds., *Necessary Truth: A Book of Readings,* New York: Random, 1969, pp. 44–64. Chapter 2 reprinted in this volume.

Pasch, Alan. *Experience and the Analytic,* Chapters 1, 2, Chicago: University of Chicago Press, 1958.

Quine, Willard Van Orman. *From A Logical Point of View,* Chapter 2, pp. 20–46 ("Two Dogmas of Empiricism"), Cambridge, Mass.: Harvard University Press, 1953. Reprinted in L. W. Sumner and John Woods, eds., *Necessary Truth: A Book of Readings,* New York: Random, 1969, pp. 116–159. Also reprinted in this volume.

———. *Word and Object,* Chapter 2, Cambridge, Mass.: Technology Press of the M.I.T., 1960.

Reichenback, Hans. *Rise of Scientific Philosophy,* Chapters 2, 3, Berkeley and Los Angeles: University of California Press, 1951.

Russell, Bertrand. *A Critical Exposition of the Philosophy of Leibniz* (1900), Chapters 2, 3, London: Allen and Unwin, 1958.

———. *The Analysis of Matter,* Chapters 17, London: Allen and Unwin, 1954, pp. 169–178. Excerpts reprinted in this volume.

———. *Introduction to Mathematical Philosophy,* Chapters 1, 2, 13, 14, 18, London: Allen and Unwin, 1919, 1960.

———. *The Problems of Philosophy* (1912), Chapters 7, 8, New York: Oxford University Press, 1959.

Sellars, Wilfrid. *Science, Perception and Reality,* Chapter 10, New York: Humanities Press, 1963.

Sigwart, Christoph von. *Logik* (1st German edition 1873–1878; translated 1895), Chapter 18, Tübingen: J. C. B. Mahr, 1911.

Stace, Walter Terence. *Theory of Knowledge and Existence,* Chapter 13, Oxford: Clarendon, 1932.

Sumner, L. W., and John Woods, eds. *Necessary Truth: A Book of Readings,* New York: Random, 1969.

Von Mises, Richard, *Positivism,* Chapters 9–11, Cambridge, Mass.: Harvard University Press, 1951, 1956.

Von Wright, Georg Henrik. *Logical Studies,* Chapters 1, 2, London: Routledge and Kegan Paul, 1957.

Waismann, Friedrich. R. Harré, ed., *Principles of Linguistic Philosophy,* Chapter 3 ("Is There A Priori Knowledge?"), New York: St. Martin's, 1965, pp. 44–67.

Walsh, William Henry. *Reason and Experience,* Chapter 3, Oxford: Clarendon, 1947.

Weinberg, Julius Rudolph. *An Examination of Logical Positivism,* Chapter 2, New York: Harcourt, 1936.

White, Morton Gabriel. *Toward Reunion in Philosophy,* Part II, Chapters 7–9, Cambridge, Mass.: Harvard University Press, 1956, pp. 113–163.

Wilson, John Cook. *Statement and Inference,* Part II, Chapter 11 (Vol. I, pp. 231 ff.), Oxford: Clarendon, 1926.

Wittgenstein, Ludwig. *Remarks on the Foundations of Mathematics,* Oxford: Blackwell, 1956.

———. *Tractatus Logico-Philosophicus* (1922), Chapter 6, London: Routledge and Kegan Paul, 1963.

Woods, John. See L. W. Sumner and John Woods, eds., *Necessary Truth: A Book of Readings.*

Articles

Ajdukiewicz, Kazimiery. "Le problème du fondement des propositions analytiques," *Studia Logica,* VIII (1958), 259–272.

Aldrich, Virgil C. "Analytic *A Posteriori* Propositions," *Analysis,* XXVIII, 6 (June 1968), 200–202.

———. "The Last Word on Being Red and Blue All Over," *Philosophical Studies,* V, 1 (January 1954), 5–10.

——— "Logically Necessary *A Posteriori* Propositions," *Analysis,* XXIX (March 1969), 140–142.

Alexander, H. G. "Necessary Truth," *Mind,* LXVI, 264 (October 1957), 507–521.

Allaire, Edwin B. "Tractatus 6.3751," *Analysis,* XIX (April 1959), 100–105.

Ambrose, Alice."Self-Contradictory Suppositions," *Mind,* LIII, 209 (January 1944), 48–59.

Aune, Bruce. "Is There an Analytic *A Priori?" Journal of Philosophy,* LX, 11 (May 1963), 281–291.

Ayer, A. J. "Internal Relations," *Proceedings of the Aristotelian Society, Supplementary Volume* XIV (1935), 173–185. Symposium with Gilbert Ryle, 154–172.

————. See Max Black *et al.,* "Truth by Convention."

Baier, K. "Contradiction and Absurdity," *Analysis,* XV, 2 (December 1954), 31–40.

Bar-Hillel, Y. "Bolzano's Definition of Analytic Propositions," *Theoria,* XVI, 2 (1950), 91–117.

Barker, Stephen. "Are Some Analytic Propositions Contingent?" *Journal of Philosophy,* LXIII, 20 (October 1966), 637–639. Symposium with Milton Fisk, "Analyticity and Conceptual Revision," 627–637, and Sue Larson, "Analyticity and Impropriety," 640–642.

Basson, A. H. "Logic and Fact," *Analysis,* VIII, 6 (1948), 81–87.

Beard, Robert W. "Analyticity, Informativeness, and the Incompatibility of Colors," *Logique et Analyse,* X (June 1967), 211–217.

Beck, Lewis White. "Can Kant's Synthetic Judgments Be Made Analytic?" *Kant-Studien,* XLVII, 2 (1955), 168–181. Reprinted in Lewis White Beck, *Studies in the Philosophy of Kant,* New York: Bobbs-Merrill, 1965, pp. 74–91.

————. "Kant's Theory of Definition," *Philosophical Review,* LXV (1956), 179–191. Reprinted in Lewis White Beck, *Studies in the Philosophy of Kant,* New York: Bobbs-Merrill, 1965, pp. 61–73.

————. "On the Meta-Semantics of the Problem of the Synthetic *A Priori," Mind,* LXVI, 262 (April 1957), 228–232. Reprinted in Lewis White Beck, *Studies in the Philosophy of Kant,* New York: Bobbs-Merrill, pp. 92–98.

Benardete, José A. "The Analytic *A Posteriori* and the Foundations of Metaphysics," *Journal of Philosophy,* LV, 12 (June 1958), 503–514.

————. "Is There a Problem About Logical Possibility?" *Mind,* LXXI, 283 (July 1962), 342–352.

Bennett, Jonathan F. "A Myth About Logical Necessity," *Analysis,* XXI, 3 (January 1961), 59–63.

————. "Analytic-Synthetic," *Proceedings of the Aristotelian*

Society, LIX (1958/1959), 163–188. Reprinted in L. W. Sumner and John Woods, eds., *Necessary Truth: A Book of Readings,* New York: Random, 1969, pp. 160–184.

Bergmann, Gustav. "Analyticity," *Theoria,* XXIV, 2 (1958), 71–93. Also in Gustav Bergmann, *Meaning and Existence,* Chapter 3, Madison, Wisconsin: University of Wisconsin Press, 1960, pp. 73–90.

Bird, G. H. "Analytic and Synthetic," *Philosophical Quarterly,* XI, 44 (1961), 227–237.

Black, Max. "Necessary Statements and Rules," *Philosophical Review,* LXVII (1958), 313–341. Reprinted in Max Black, *Models and Metaphors: Studies in Language and Philosophy,* Ithaca, N.Y.: Cornell University Press, 1962, pp. 64–94.

————, A. J. Ayer, and C. H. Whiteley, "Truth by Convention," *Analysis,* IV (December 1936), 17–32.

Bohnert, H. G. "Carnap on Definition and Analyticity," in Paul A. Schilpp, ed., *The Philosophy of Rudolf Carnap,* Chapter 13, La Salle, Ill.: Open Court, 1963, pp. 407–430.

Bradley, Raymond D. "Geometry and Necessary Truth," *Philosophical Review,* LXXIII, 1 (January 1964), 59–75.

Britton, Karl. "Are Necessary Truths True by Convention?" *Proceedings of the Aristotelian Society, Supplementary Volume* XXI (1947), 78–103. Symposium with J. O. Urmson, 104–117, and W. C. Kneale, 118–133.

————. "The Nature of Arithmetic—A Reconsideration of Mill's Views," *Proceedings of the Aristotelian Society,* XLVIII (1947/1948), 1–12.

Broad, C. D. "Are There Synthetic *A Priori* Truths?" *Proceedings of the Aristotelian Society, Supplementary Volume* XV (1936), 102–117.

————. "Kant's Theory of Mathematical and Philosophical Reasoning," *Proceedings of the Aristotelian Society,* XLII (1941/1942), 1–24.

————, A. J. D. Porteous, and R. Jackson. "Are There Synthetic *A Priori* Truths?" *Proceedings of the Aristotelian Society,* XV (1936), 102–153.

Bunge, Mario. "Analyticity Redefined," *Mind,* LXX, 278 (April 1961), 239–245.

Butts, Robert E. "Necessary Truth in Whewell's Theory of Science," *American Philosophical Quarterly,* XI (July 1965), 161–181.

Campbell, C. A. "Contradiction: 'Law' or 'Convention'?" *Analysis*, XVIII, 4 (March 1958), 73–76.

———. "Contradiction: Comment upon Professor Henze's Criticism," *Analysis*, XXII, 2 (December 1961), 28–30.

———. "Contradiction Again: Comment upon Professor Henze's Rejoinder," *Analysis*, XXII, 6 (June 1962), 145–147.

Carnap, Rudolf. "Formal and Factual Science," in Herbert Feigl and May Brodbeck, eds., *Readings in the Philosophy of Science*, New York: Appleton-Century-Crofts, 1953, pp. 123–128. Originally in *Erkenntis*, 5, (1934).

———. "Meaning Postulates," *Philosophical Studies*, III, 5 (October 1952), 65–73. Reprinted in Rudolf Carnap, *Meaning and Necessity: A Study in Semantics and Modal Logic*, 2nd ed., Appendix B, Chicago: University of Chicago Press, 1956, pp. 222–229.

———. "The Old and the New Logic," trans. from the German in A. J. Ayer, ed., *Logical Positivism*, Glencoe, Illinois: Free Press, 1959, pp. 133–146. Originally "Die Alte und die neue Logik," *Erkenntis*, I (1930–1931). Also Vol. IX of *Annalen der Philosophie*.

———. "Testability and Meaning," *Philosophy of Science*, III (1936), 419–471, and IV (1937), 1–40. Part reprinted in Herbert Feigl and May Brodbeck, eds., *Readings in the Philosophy of Science*, New York: Appleton-Century-Crofts, 1953, pp. 47–92; and in Robert R. Ammerman, ed., *Classics of Analytic Philosophy*, New York: McGraw-Hill, 1965, pp. 130–195.

Castaneda, Hector Neri. "Analytical Propositions, Definitions and the *A Priori*," *Ratio*, II, 1 (August 1959), 80–101.

———. " '7+5=12' as a Synthetic Proposition," *Philosophy and Phenomenological Research*, XXI, 2 (December 1960), 141–158.

Chihara, Charles. "On the Possibility of Completing an Infinite Process," *Philosophical Review*, LXXIV, 1 (January 1965), 74–87.

Chisholm, Roderick M. "Reason and the *A Priori*," in Richard Schlatter, ed., *Philosophy*, Englewood Cliffs, N.J.: Prentice-Hall, Princeton Studies in Humanistic Scholarship, 1964, pp. 287–311.

Cobitz, J. L. See J. Wild and J. L. Cobitz, "On the Distinction between the Analytic and the Synthetic."

Coles, Norman. "Self-Evidence," *Analysis,* XXIV, 3 (January 1964), 58–62.

Copi, Irving M. "Analytical Philosophy and Analytical Propositions," *Philosophical Studies,* IV, 6 (December 1953), 87–93.

————. "Modern Logic and the Synthetic *A Priori,*" *Journal of Philosophy,* XLVI, 8 (April 1949), 243–245.

Donnellan, Keith. "Necessity and Criteria," *Journal of Philosophy,* LIX, 22 (October 1962), 647–658.

Ebersole, Frank B. "On Certain Confusions in the Analytic-Synthetic Distinction," *Journal of Philosophy,* LIII, 16 (August 1956), 485–494.

Edwards, Paul. "Do Necessary Propositions 'Mean Nothing'?" *Journal of Philosophy,* XLVI, 15 (July 1949), 457–468.

————. "Necessary Propositions and the Future," *Journal of Philosophy,* XLVI, 6 (March 1949), 155–157.

Emmet, Dorothy. " 'That's That': Or Some Uses of Tautology," *Philosophy,* XXXVII, 139 (January 1962), 15–24.

Ewing, A. C. "The Linguistic Theory of *A Priori* Propositions," *Proceedings of the Aristotelian Society,* XL (1939/1940), 207–244.

Ferré, Frederick. "Colour Incompatibility and Language-Games," *Mind,* LXX, 277 (January 1961), 90–94.

Fisk, Milton. "Analyticity and Conceptual Revision," *Journal of Philosophy,* LXIII, 20 (October 1966), 627–637. Symposium with Stephen Barker, "Are Some Analytic Propositions Contingent?" 637–639, and Sue Larson, "Analyticity and Impropriety," 640–642.

Gahringer, Robert F. "Analytic Propositions and Philosophical Truths," *Journal of Philosophy,* LX, 17 (August 1963), 481–502.

Garver, Newton. "Analyticity and Grammar," *Monist,* LI (July 1967), 397–425.

Gasking, D. A. T. "Mathematics and the World," *Australasian Journal of Philosophy,* XVIII, 2 (September 1940), 97–116. Reprinted in Paul Benacerraf and Hilary Putnam, eds., *Philosophy of Mathematics,* Englewood Cliffs, N.J.: Prentice-Hall, 1964, pp. 390–403.

Gewirth, Alan. "The Distinction between Analytic and Synthetic Truths," *Journal of Philosophy,* L, 14 (July 1953), 397–425.

Goldstein, Leon J. "On Anything Whatever," *Mind,* LXXIV, 294 (April 1965), 236–239.

Grice, H. P., and P. F. Strawson. "In Defense of a Dogma," *Philosophical Review,* LXV (1956), 141–158. Reprinted in Robert R. Ammerman, ed., *Classics of Analytic Philosophy,* New York: McGraw-Hill, 1965, pp. 340–352; L. W. Sumner and John Woods, *Necessary Truth: A Book of Readings,* New York: Random, 1969, pp. 141–159. Also reprinted in this volume.

Hackett, Stuart C. "Contemporary Philosophy and the Analytic-Synthetic Dichotomy," *International Philosophical Quarterly,* VII (September 1967), 413–440.

Hahn, Hans. "Logic, Mathematics and Knowledge of Nature," in A. J. Ayer, ed., *Logical Positivism,* Glencoe, III.: Free Press, 1959, pp. 147–161. Originally sections 1–4 of "Logik, Mathematik und Naturerkennen" (pamphlet), "Einheitswissenschaft" series, Vol. II Vienna: 1933.

Hallett, H. F. "The *A Priori,*" *Proceedings of the Aristotelian Society, Supplementary Volume* XII, 1933, 150–177. Symposium with L. S. Stebbing, 178–197, and J. H. Muirhead, 199–219.

Hamlyn, D. W. "Analytic Truths," *Mind,* LXV, 259 (July 1956), 359–367.

———. "On Necessary Truth," *Mind,* LXX, 280 (October 1961), 514–525.

Hampshire, Stuart. "Logical Necessity," *Philosophy,* XXIII, 87 (October 1948), 332–345.

Hanson, Norwood Russell. "Imagining the Impossible," *Analysis,* XIX, 4 (March 1959), 86–92.

———. "Justifying Analytic Claims," *Analysis,* XXIII, 5 (April 1963) 103–105.

———. "The Very Idea of a Synthetic-Apriori," *Mind,* LXXI, 284 (October 1962), 521–524. Reprinted in L. W. Sumner and John Woods, eds., *Necessary Truth: A Book of Readings,* New York: Random, 1969, 65–70.

Hardie, C. D. "The Necessity of *A Priori* Propositions," *Proceedings of the Aristotelian Society,* XXXVIII (1937/1938), 47–60.

Hay, W. H., and J. R. Weinberg. "Concerning Allegedly Necessary Nonanalytic Propositions," *Philosophical Studies,* II, 2 (February 1951), 17–21.

Hempel, Carl G. "Geometry and Empirical Science," *American Mathematical Monthly,* LII (January 1945), 7–17.

―――. "Implications of Carnap's Work for the Philosophy of Science," in Paul A. Schilpp, ed., *The Philosophy of Rudolph Carnap,* La Salle, Ill.: Open Court, 1964, pp. 685–707.

―――. "On the Nature of Mathematical Truth," *American Mathematical Monthly,* LII (December 1945), 543–556. Reprinted in Paul Benacerraf and Hilary Putnam, eds., *Philosophy of Mathematics,* Englewood Cliffs, N.J.: Prentice-Hall, 1964, pp. 366–381; Herbert Feigl and May Brodbeck, eds., *Readings in the Philosophy of Science,* New York: Appleton-Century-Crofts, 1953, pp. 148–162; Herbert Feigl and Wilfrid Sellars, eds., *Readings in Philosophical Analysis,* New York: Appleton-Century-Crofts, 1949, pp. 222–237.

Henze, Donald F. "Aldrich's Monstrous Supposition," *Analysis,* XXIX, 4 (March 1969), 137–139.

―――. "Contradiction," *Analysis,* XXII, 2 (December 1961), 25–28.

―――. "Contradiction Again: A Rejoinder to Professor Campbell," *Analysis,* XXII, 6 (June 1962), 142–144.

Herburt, G. K. "The Analytic and the Synthetic," *Philosophy of Science,* XXVI, No. 2 (1959), 104–113.

Hintikka, Jaakko. "Are Logical Truths Analytic?" *Philosophical Review,* LXXIV, 2 (April 1965), 178–203. Reprinted in L. W. Sumner and John Woods, eds., *Necessary Truth: A Book of Readings,* New York: Random, 1969, pp. 94–115.

Hofstadter, Albert. "Causality and Necessity," *Journal of Philosophy,* XLVI, 9 (April 1949), 257–270.

―――. "The Myth of the Whole," *Journal of Philosophy,* LI, 14 (July 1954), 397–417.

―――. "Six Necessities," *Journal of Philosophy,* LIV, 20 (September 1957), 597–613.

Hook, Sidney. "Experimental Logic," *Mind,* XL (1931), 424–438.

Ihrig, Ann H. "Remarks on Logical Necessity and Future Contingencies," *Mind,* LXXIV, 294 (April 1965), 215–228.

Jackson, R. "Are There Analytic Propositions?" *Proceedings of the Aristotelian Society,* XXXIX (1938/1939), 185–206.

―――. "Are There Synthetic *A Priori* Truths?" *Proceedings of the Aristotelian Society, Supplementary Volume* XV (1936), 141–153.

Jackson, R. See C. D. Broad *et al.,* "Are There Synthetic *A Priori* Truths?"

Johnson, Oliver A. "Denial of the Synthetic *A Priori,*" *Philosophy,* XXXV, 134 (July 1960), 255–264.

Katz, Jerrold J. "Analyticity and Contradiction in Natural Language," in Jerrold J. Katz and Jerry A. Fodor, *The Structure of Language,* Chapter 20, Englewood Cliffs, N.J.: Prentice-Hall, 1964, pp. 519–543.

————. "Some Remarks on Quine on Analyticity," *Journal of Philosophy,* LXIV, 2 (February 1967), 36–52. Reprinted in L. W. Sumner and John Woods, eds., *Necessary Truth: A Book of Readings,* New York: Random, 1969, pp. 185–203.

————. "Unpalatable Recipes for Buttering Parsnips," *Journal of Philosophy,* LXV, 2 (January 1968), 29–45.

Kaufman, Arnold S. "The Analytic and the Synthetic," *Philosophical Review,* LXII, 3 (July 1953), 421–426.

Keene, G. B. "Analytic Statements and Mathematical Truth," *Analysis,* XVI, 4 (March 1956), 86–90.

Kemeny, John G. "A New Approach to Semantics," *Journal of Symbolic Logic,* XXI, 1 (March 1956), 1–27, 149–161.

————. "Analyticity versus Fuzziness," *Synthese,* XV, 1 (March 1963), 57–79.

Kneale, William C. "Are Necessary Truths True by Convention?" *Proceedings of the Aristotelian Society, Supplementary Volume* XXI (1947), 118–133. Symposium with Karl Britton, 78–103, and J. O. Urmson, 104–117.

————. "Truths of Logic," *Proceedings of the Aristotelian Society,* XLVI (1945/1946), 207–234.

Koppelmann. "Kant's Lehre vom analytischen Urtheil," *Philosophische Monatschefte,* XXI (Heidelberg: 1885), 65–101.

Krishna, Daya. "The Synthetic *A Priori*—Some Considerations," *Philosophy,* XXXVI, 137 (April–July 1961), 211–215.

Kühnemann, E. "Analytisch und Synthetisch," *Archiv fur systematische Philosophie* (1895), 165–203.

Lachièze-Rey, P. "Reflexions historiques et critiques sur la possibilité des jugements synthetiques *a priori,*" *Revue Internationale de Philosophie,* VIII, No. 4 (1954), 358–370.

Lake, Beryl. "Necessary and Contingent Statements," *Analysis*, XII, 5 (1952), 115–122.

Langford, C. H. "A Proof that Synthetic *A Priori* Propositions Exist," *Journal of Philosophy*, XLVI, 1 (January 1949), 20–24.

Larson, Sue. "Analyticity and Impropriety," *Journal of Philosophy*, LXIII, 20 (October 1966), 640–642. Symposium with Milton Fisk, "Analyticity and Conceptual Revision," 627–637, and Stephen Barker, "Are Some Analytic Propositions Contingent?" 637–639.

Lazerowitz, Morris. "Are Self-Contradictory Expressions Meaningless?" *Philosophical Review*, LVIII, 6 (1949), 563–584. Also in Morris Lazerowitz, *The Structure of Metaphysics*, Chapter 11, London: Routledge and Kegan Paul, 1955, pp. 231–253.

————. "Necessary and Contingent Truths," *Philosophical Review*, XLV, 3 (May 1936), 268–282.

Leibniz, Gottfried Wilhelm. "Necessary and Contingent Truths," in T. V. Smith and Marjorie Grene, eds., *From Descartes to Kant*, Chicago: University of Chicago Press, 1940, pp. 346–352. Also reprinted in this volume.

Levison, A. B. "Wittgenstein and Logical Laws," *Philosophical Quarterly*, XIV, 57 (1964), 345–354.

Lewis, C. I. "The Pragmatic Conception of the *A Priori*," *Journal of Philosophy*, XX, 7 (March 1923), 169–177. Reprinted in Herbert Feigl and Wilfrid Sellars, eds., *Readings in Philosophical Analysis*, New York: Appleton-Century-Crofts, 1949, pp. 286–296; Ernest Nagel and Richard B. Brandt, eds., *Meaning and Knowledge*, New York: Harcourt, 1965, pp. 221–227.

Lewy, Casimir. "Logical Necessity," *Philosophical Review*, XLIX, 1 (January 1940), 62–68.

————. See Gilbert Ryle *et al.*, "Why Are the Calculuses of Logic and Arithmetic Applicable to Reality?"

Liu, Shih-Chao. "On the Analytic and the Synthetic," *Philosophical Review*, LXV (1956), 218–328.

Locke, Don. "The Necessity of Analytic Truths," *Philosophy*, XLIV (January 1969), 12–32.

Long, Peter. "Modality and Tautology," *Proceedings of the Aristotelian Society*, LX (1959/1960), 27–36.

MacDonald, Margaret. "Necessary Propositions," *Analysis*, VII (1940), 45–51.

McGee, C. D. "Pre-Ceremonial Relations," *Philosophical Quarterly,* XIII (1963), 125–133.

Malcolm, Norman. "Are Necessary Propositions Really Verbal?" *Mind,* XLIX, 194 (April 1940), 189–203.

————. "The Nature of Entailment," *Mind,* XLIX, 195 (July 1940), 333–347.

Manser, Anthony. "How Did Kant Define Analytic?" *Analysis,* XXVIII (June 1968), 197–199.

Marc-Wogau, Konrad. "Kant's Lehre vom analytischen Urteil," *Theoria,* XVII, 1–3 (1951), 140–154.

Martin, R. M. "On 'Analytic,'" *Philosophical Studies,* III, 3 (April 1952), 42–47.

Mates, Benson. "Analytic Sentences," *Philosophical Review,* LX, 4 (October 1951), 525–534.

Maxwell, G. "The Necessary and the Contingent," in Herbert Feigl and G. Maxwell, eds., *Minnesota Studies in the Philosophy of Science,* III, Minneapolis: University of Minnesota Press, 1962, pp. 398–404.

Moore, G. E. "Necessity," *Mind,* IX (1900), 289–304.

Moravcsik, J. M. E. "The Analytic and the Nonempirical," *Journal of Philosophy,* LXII, 16 (August 1965), 415–429.

Muirhead, J. H. "The *A Priori,*" *Proceedings of the Aristotelian Society, Supplementary Volume* XII (1933), 199–219. Symposium with H. F. Hallett, 150–177, and L. S. Stebbing, 178–197.

Nagel, Ernest. "Logic without Ontology," in Yervant Hovhannes Krikorian, *Naturalism and the Human Spirit,* Chapter 4, New York: Columbia University Press, 1944. Also in Paul Benacerraf and Hilary Putnam, eds., *Philosophy of Mathematics,* Englewood Cliffs, N.J.: Prentice-Hall, 1964, pp. 302–321; Herbert Feigl and Wilfrid Sellars, eds., *Readings in Philosophical Analysis,* New York: Appleton-Century-Crofts, 1949, pp. 191–210.

Nell, Edward J. "The Hardness of the Logical 'Must,'" *Analysis,* XXI, 3 (January 1961), 68–72.

Nelson, Everett J. "Contradiction and the Presupposition of Existence," *Mind,* LV, 220 (October 1946), 319–327.

Nelson, J. O. "y-Propositions," *Philosophical Studies,* XII (1961), 65–72.

O'Connor, D. J. "Incompatible Properties," *Analysis,* XV, 5 (April 1955), 109–117.

Odegard, Douglas. "The Discovery of Analytic Truth," *Philosophy and Phenomenological Research,* XXVI, (December 1965), 248–252.

Pap, Arthur. "Are All Necessary Propositions Analytic?" *Philosophical Review,* LVIII (1949), 299–320.

————. "The Different Kinds of *A Priori,*" *Philosophical Review,* LIII, 5 (September 1944), 465–484.

————. "Logic and the Synthetic *A Priori,*" *Philosophy and Phenomenological Research,* X (1949/1950), 500–514.

————. "Logical Nonsense," *Philosophy and Phenomenological Research,* IX (1948/1949), 269–283.

————. "Necessary Propositions and Linguistic Rules," *Semantica,* 1955.

————. "On the Meaning of Necessity," *Journal of Philosophy,* XL, 17 (August 1943), 449–458.

Peach, Bernard. "A Nondescriptive Theory of the Analytic," *Philosophical Review,* LXI (1952), 349–367.

Pears, David F. "Incompatibilities of Colors," in Antony Garrard Newton Flew, ed., *Logic and Language,* Second Series, Oxford: Blackwell, 1953, pp. 112–122.

————. "The Incongruity of Counterparts," *Mind,* LXI, 241 (January 1952), 78–81.

————. "Synthetic Necessary Truth," *Mind,* LIX, 234 (April 1950), 199–208.

Pollock, John L. "Implication and Analyticity," *Journal of Philosophy,* LXII, 6 (March 1965), 150–157.

————. "The Logic of Logical Necessity," *Logique et Analyse,* X (December 1967), 307–323.

————. "Mathematical Proof," *American Philosophical Quarterly,* IV (July 1967), 238–244.

Popper, K. R. See Gilbert Ryle *et al.,* "Why Are The Calculuses of Logic and Arithmetic Applicable to Reality?"

Porteous, A. J. D. See C. D. Broad *et al.,* "Are There Synthetic *A Priori* Truths?"

Putnam, Hilary. "The Analytic and the Synthetic," in Herbert Feigl and G. Maxwell, eds., *Minnesota Studies in the Philosophy of Science,* Vol. III, Minneapolis: University of Minnesota Press, 1962, pp. 358–397.

————. "It Ain't Necessarily So," *Journal of Philosophy,* LIX, 22 (October 1962), 658–671.

Putnam, Hilary. "Reds, Greens, and Logical Analysis," *Philosophical Review,* LXV (1956), 206–217. Reprinted in L. W. Sumner and John Woods, eds., *Necessary Truth: A Book of Readings,* New York: Random, 1969, pp. 71–83.

Quine, Willard Van Orman. "Carnap and Logical Truth," in Paul A. Schilpp, ed., *The Philosophy of Rudolf Carnap,* Chapter 12, La Salle, III. Open Court, 1963, pp. 385–406.

————. "On a Suggestion of Katz," *Journal of Philosophy,* LXIV, 2 (February 1967), 52–54. Reprinted in L. W. Sumner and John Woods, eds., *Necessary Truth: A Book of Readings,* New York: Random, 1969, pp. 204–206.

————. "Truth by Convention," in *Philosophical Essays for Alfred North Whitehead* (Copyright by Otis H. Lee), New York: Russell and Russell, 1936, 1967, pp. 90–124. Also in Paul Benacerraf and Hilary Putnam, eds., *Philosophy of Mathematics,* Englewood Cliffs, N.J.: Prentice-Hall, 1964, pp. 322–345; Herbert Feigl and Wilfrid Sellars, eds., *Readings in Philosophical Analysis,* New York: Appleton-Century-Crofts, 1949, pp. 250–273.

————. "Two Dogmas of Empiricism," *Philosophical Review,* CX, 1 (January 1951), 20–43. Also in Willard Van Orman Quine, *From A Logical Point of View,* Chapter 2, Cambridge, Mass.: Harvard University Press, 1953, pp. 20–46; Robert R. Ammerman, ed., *Classics of Analytic Philosophy,* New York: McGraw-Hill, 1965, pp. 196–213; Paul Benacerraf and Hilary Putnam, eds., *Philosophy of Mathematics,* Englewood Cliffs, N.J.: Prentice-Hall, 1964, pp. 346–365.

Quinton, A. M. "The *A Priori* and the Analytic," *Proceedings of the Aristotelian Society,* LXIV (1963/1964), 31–54.

Radford, Colin. "Incompatibilities of Colours," *Philosophical Quarterly,* XV (1965), 207–219.

————. "The Insolubility of the Red-Green Problem," *Analysis,* XXIII, 3 (January 1963), 68–71.

Rankin, K. W. "Rule and Reality," *Philosophical Quarterly,* XI, 43 (1961), 145–157.

Reid, John R. "Analytic Statements in Semiosis," *Mind,* LII, 208 (October 1943), 314–330.

Richman, Robert J. "Why Are Synthetic *A Priori* Judgments Necessary?" *Theoria,* XXX, 1 (1964), 5–20.

Robinson, Richard. "Necessary Propositions," *Mind,* LXVII, 267 (July 1958), 289–304.

Rosenthal, Sandra B. "The Analytic, the Synthetic, and C. I. Lewis," *Tulane Studies in Philosophy,* XVII (1968), 115–123.

Rozebloom, William W. "The Logic of Color Words," *Philosophical Review,* LXVII (1958), 353–366.

Ryle, Gilbert. "Internal Relations," *Proceedings of the Aristotelian Society, Supplementary Volume* XIV (1935), 154–172. Symposium with A. J. Ayer, 173–185.

————, Casimir Lewy, and K. R. Popper. "Why Are the Calculuses of Logic and Arithmetic Applicable to Reality?" symposium in *Proceedings of the Aristotelian Society, Supplementary Volume* XX (1946), 20–60.

Rynin, David. "The Dogma of Logical Pragmatism," *Mind,* LXV, 259 (July 1956), 379–391.

Schlick, Moritz. "Gibt es ein materiales *a priori?*" ("Is There a Factual *A Priori?*"), *Wissenshaftlicher Jahresbericht der Philosophischen Gesellschaft an der Universität zu Wein für das Vereinsjahr* (1930/1931). Reprinted in Herbert Feigl and Wilfrid Sellars, eds., *Readings in Philosophical Analysis,* New York: Appleton-Century-Crofts, 1949, pp. 277 285.

Sellars, Wilfrid. "Inference and Meaning," *Mind,* LXII, 247 (July 1953), 313–338.

————. "Is There a Synthetic *A Priori?*" *Philosophy of Science,* XX, 2 (1953), 121–138.

Shwayder, David S. "Self-Defeating Pronouncements," *Analysis,* XVI, 4 (March 1956), 74–85.

Sibajiban. "Can the Law of Contradiction Be Stated?," *Analysis,* XXI, 5 (April 1961), 101–105.

————. "The Self-Contradictory and the Inconceivable," *Analysis* Supplement XXIV (January 1964), 99–103.

Sloman, Aaron. "Colour Incompatibilities and Analyticity," *Analysis* Supplement XXIV (January 1964), 104–119.

————. " 'Necessary,' 'A Priori' and 'Analytic,' " *Analysis,* XXVI (October 1965), 12–16.

Smart, J. J. C. "Incompatible Colors," *Philosophical Studies,* X, 3 (April 1959), 39–42.

Sommers, Fred. "Meaning Relations and the Analytic," *Journal of Philosophy,* LX, 18 (August 1963), 524–534.

Sprigge, T. "Internal and External Properties," *Mind,* LXXI, 282 (April 1962), 197–212.

Srzednicki, J. "Incompatibility Statements," *Australasian Journal of Philosophy,* XL, 2 (August 1962), 178–186.

Stebbing, L. S. "The *A Priori,*" *Proceedings of the Aristotelian Society, Supplementary Volume* XII (1933), 178–197. Symposium with H. F. Hallett, 150–177, and J. H. Muirhead, 199–219.

Stegmuller, W. "Der Begriff des synthetischen Urteils a priori und die moderne Logik," *Zeitschrift fur philosophische Forschung,* VIII, 4 (1954), 535–563.

Stenius, Erik. "Are True Numerical Statements Analytic or Synthetic?" *Philosophical Review,* LXXIV, 3 (July 1965), 357–372.

Strawson, P.F. "Propositions, Concepts and Logical Truths," *Philosophical Quarterly,* VII, 26 (1957), 15–25.

―――. See H. P. Grice and P. F. Strawson, "In Defense of a Dogma."

Stroud, Barry. "Wittgenstein and Logical Necessity," *Philosophical Review,* LXXIV, 4 (October 1965), 504–518.

Toulmin, Stephen. "A Defense of Synthetic Necessary Truth," *Mind,* LVIII, 230 (April 1949), 164–177.

Urmson, J. O. "Are Necessary Truths True by Convention?" *Proceedings of the Aristotelian Society, Supplementary Volume* XXI (1947), 104–117. Symposium with Karl Britton, 78–103, and W. C. Kneale, 118–133.

van der Waerden, B. L. "Synthetische Urteile a priori," *Acta Philosophica Fennica,* 18 (1965), 277–291.

Waismann, Friedrich. "Analytic-Synthetic (I)," *Analysis,* X, 2 (December 1949), 25–40.

―――. "Analytic-Synthetic (II)," *Analysis,* XI, 2 (December 1950), 25–38.

―――. "Analytic-Synthetic (III)," *Analysis,* XI, 3 (January 1951), 49–61.

―――. "Analytic-Synthetic (IV)," *Analysis,* XI, 6 (June 1951), 115–124.

―――. "Analytic-Synthetic (V)," *Analysis,* XIII, 1 (October 1952), 1–14.

―――. "Analytic-Synthetic (VI)," *Analysis,* XIII, 4 (March 1953), 73–89.

Walsh, W. H. "Analytic-Synthetic," *Proceedings of the Aristotelian Society,* X (1953/1954), 77–96.

Wang, Hao. "Notes on the Analytic-Synthetic Distinction," *Theoria*, XXI, 2–3 (1955), 158–178.

Watkins, J. W. N. "Between Analytic and Empirical," *Philosophy*, XXXII, 121 (April 1957), 112–131.

Weinberg, J. R. See W. H. Hay and J. R. Weinberg, "Concerning Allegedly Necessary Nonanalytic Propositions."

Weitz, Morris. "Analytic Statements," *Mind*, LXIII, 252 (October 1954), 487–494.

White, Morton G. "A Finitistic Approach to Philosophical Theses," *Philosophical Review*, LX, 3 (July 1951), 299–316.

———. "The Analytic and the Synthetic: An Untenable Dualism," in Sidney Hook, ed., *John Dewey, Philosopher of Science and Freedom; A Symposium*, New York: Dial, 1950, pp. 316–330. Also in Leonard Linsky, ed., *Semantics and the Philosophy of Language*, Urbana, Ill.: University of Illinois Press, 1952, pp. 272–286.

Whiteley, C. H. See Max Black *et al.*, "Truth by Convention."

Wild, J., and J. L. Cobitz. "On the Distinction between the Analytic and the Synthetic," *Philosophy and Phenomenological Research*, VIII (1947/1948), 651–667.

Williams, Donald Cary. "Analysis, Analytic Propositions, and Real Definitions," *Analysis*, III, 5 (June 1936), 75–80. Reprinted in Donald Cary Williams, *Principles of Empirical Realism*, Springfield, Ill.: Charles C. Thomas, 1966, pp. 4–11.

———. "The Nature and Variety of the A Priori," *Analysis*, V, 6 (1938), 85–94.

———. "Necessary Facts," *Review of Metaphysics*, XVI, 4 (June 1963), 601–626.

Wilson, N. L. "Linguistic Butter and Philosophical Parsnips," *Journal of Philosophy*, LXIV, 2 (February 1967), 55–67.

Winch, Peter. "Necessary and Contingent Truths," *Analysis*, XIII, 3 (January 1953), 52–60.

Woods, John. "The Contradiction Exterminator," *Analysis*, XXV, 3 (January 1965), 49–53.

Basic Problems in Philosophy Series

A. I. Melden and Stanley Munsat
University of California, Irvine
General Editors

Morality and the Law
Richard A. Wasserstrom

Introduction   On Liberty, *John Stuart Mill*   Morals and the Criminal Law, *Lord Patrick Devlin*   Immorality and Treason, *H. L. A. Hart*   Lord Devlin and the Enforcement of Morals, *Ronald Dworkin*   Sins and Crimes, *A. R. Louch*   Morals Offenses and the Model Penal Code, *Louis B. Schwartz*   Paternalism, *Gerald Dworkin*   Four cases involving the enforcement of morality   Bibliography

War and Morality
Richard A. Wasserstrom

Introduction   The Moral Equivalent of War, *William James*   The Morality of Obliteration Bombing, *John C. Ford, S.J.*   War and Murder, *Elizabeth Anscombe*   Moral Judgment in Time of War, *Michael Walzer*   Pacifism: A Philosophical Analysis, *Jan Narveson*   On the Morality of War: A Preliminary Inquiry, *Richard Wasserstrom*   Judgment and Opinion, The International Tribunal, Nuremberg, Germany   Superior Orders, Nuclear Warfare, and the Dictates of Conscience, *Guenter Lewy*   Selected Bibliography